MONTH-TO-MONTH GARDENING COLORADO

A Practical Guide for Designing,
Growing and Maintaining Your
Colorado Garden

KELLI DOLECEK

MONTH-TO-MONTH GARDENING COLORADO

Copyright © 2002 3D Press, Inc. All rights reserved.
No part of this book may be used or reproduced in any manner whatsoever or stored in a database or retrieval system, without prior written permission from the publisher.

SECOND EDITION

Design Sallie Reynolds
Photography Paul Bousquet, Scott Dressel-Martin, Roger Speyer, US Dept. of Agriculture
Landscape Designs and General Information Carole Kastler, Camelot Design
Mountain Information, Mountain Landscape Design Donna Elliott, Elliott & Associates, Inc.
Whimsical Garden Information and Design Wendy Booth, Ivy Street Design
Interior Garden Illustration Fresh Ink, Lizabeth Netzel
Water Garden Illustration Debrah Binard
Editing Kathy Sullivan, Blue Skies Ahead and Dave Rich
Production Artist Sharon Noe

ISBN 1-889593-01-X

Printed in Canada

3D Press, Inc.
4340 E. Kentucky Ave., Suite 446
Denver, CO 80246
303-300-4484 (phone)
303-300-4494 (fax)
info@3dpress.net (email)

888-456-3607 (*order toll-free*)
www.3dpress.net

Library of Congress Catalog Card Number: 99-61292

INTRODUCTION

Experience counts in gardening, especially in a state such as Colorado. And that's what this newly revised edition of MONTH-TO-MONTH GARDENING COLORADO brings you – advice from gardening experts with over 125 years of Colorado gardening expertise and experience.

All of the gardening and landscaping experts in this book have seen literally thousands of Colorado gardens. Their advice is based on real-life experience, not theoretical know-how. If you have questions about your Colorado garden, they most likely have the answers. Many of your questions should be answered by this book.

MONTH-TO-MONTH GARDENING COLORADO is designed to help you in two ways. First, it quickly covers the essentials you need to know to design, grow and maintain a Colorado garden. It's geared toward people who don't have time to conduct extensive research, won't wade through long, complicated books or can't spend ten hours a week in their yard learning through trial and error. Second, the "when" in Colorado is just as important as the "how." This book is divided into 12 months that give you over 250 of the best ideas of when to grow and when to maintain your garden.

In this book, you will find a Colorado lawn calendar, a special section on trees and shrubs, and over 90 detailed tips on Colorado soil, staking, pruning, mulching, insects, weeds, watering and more.

There is information on what flowers bloom when, herbs, vegetables, roses, interior plants, perennials and annuals. Plus, there are 12 practical, simple designs for Colorado landscaping and best and worst plant lists for Colorado gardens.

This new edition of MONTH-TO-MONTH GARDENING COLORADO is for anyone who wants a straightforward path to feeling comfortable about gardening in Colorado.

LANDSCAPE AND GARDEN EXPERTS

MONTH-TO-MONTH GARDENING COLORADO EDITOR /
Ruth Stadler, Horticulturist
Ruth's specialty is diagnosing garden problems and teaching environmentally-safe gardening. She has taught over 5,000 Master Gardener volunteers and has published over 150 articles on a variety of gardening topics.

ADDITIONAL EXPERTS /

Carole Kastler, Camelot Design
303-734-1126 / carole@ecentral.com
A landscape design company with special emphasis on Xeriscape and native gardens.

Donna Elliott
Specializes in mountain landscapes, with emphasis on perennials and low-water design.

David Graham, Phase One Landscapes
303-750-6060
Phase One Landscapes is a design/build landscape renovation firm.

Debrah Binard, BCI Landscape Contractors
303-279-4821
Specializes in the use of water, native plant materials, flagstone and boulders to create unique Colorado landscapes.

Joan Franson, Consulting Rosarian
303-424-3942
Joan Franson has over 40 years of experience and expertise with roses.

Terry Rennolds, Little Eden Plantscaping
303-422-3336
Focuses on interior container plants – from atriums to single plants to sunrooms.

Thomas Tolkacz, Swingle Tree and Landscape Care Company
303-337-6200
A specialist in Colorado tree and lawn care and maintenance for over 50 years.

Wendy Booth, Ivy Street Design
303-320-0362
A landscape architecture and design company specializing in creating beautiful, practical landscapes for Colorado.

Lise Mahnke, Earth Mamas
303-232-1929
Specializes in perennials.

Jeff Sorenson, Rabbit Shadow Farms
970-667-5531
Specializes in herbs, perennials and topiaries.

ABOUT THE AUTHOR /
Kelli Dolecek is one of the people who needed, but couldn't find a book like COLORADO MONTH-TO-MONTH GARDENING. To write this book, she worked with Colorado landscape experts with over 100 years of hands-on Colorado gardening experience. Kelli is a researcher who conducts executive interviews for trade associations, making her well-qualified to compile and write the books in the Month-To-Month Gardening series. "I write these books for people like me – not a lot of time for gardening, but the desire for some satisfaction from creating a nice yard." In addition to working and writing, Kelli spends time with her husband and two sons, gardening, doing outdoor activities, reading and traveling.

TABLE OF CONTENTS

Landscape and Garden Experts	P. 2
Colorado Gardening	P. 4
February / Maintenance Tips	P. 6 - 10

SPRING

March / Maintenance Tips	P. 13 - 17
April / Maintenance Tips	P. 18 - 22
May / Maintenance Tips	P. 23 - 30

SUMMER

June / Maintenance Tips	P. 33 - 37
July / Maintenance Tips	P. 38 - 43
August / Maintenance Tips	P. 44 - 48

FALL

September / Maintenance Tips	P. 51 - 55
October / Maintenance Tips	P. 56 - 61
November / Maintenance Tips	P. 62 - 66

WINTER

December / Maintenance Tips	P. 69 - 73
January / Maintenance Tips	P. 74 - 78

DESIGNS

Water Garden	P. 80
Xeriscape™ Garden	P. 84
Kitchen Garden	P. 86
Whimsical Garden	P. 88
Rose Garden	P. 90
Container Garden	P. 92
Wildlife Garden	P. 94
Windowbox Herb Garden	P. 96
Border Flower Garden	P. 98
Interior Garden	P. 100
Mountain Garden	P. 102
Patio Garden	P. 106

HOW-TO TIPS

How To Clean Indoor Plants	P. 111
How To Compost	P. 111
How To Deadhead	P. 112
How To Keep Deer and Elk Away	P. 112
How to Deep Water	P. 113
How To Fertilize	P. 114
How To Mulch	P. 115
How To Harvest Vegetables	P. 116
How To Plant or Transplant Rose Bushes	P. 118
How To Prune	P. 119
How To Create a Miniature Orchard	P. 120
How To Plant and Transplant Trees and Shrubs	P. 120
How To Stake Trees	P. 122
How To Weed	P. 123
How To Water	P. 124
How To Amend Soil	P. 127
Colorado Insects and Diseases	P. 129

LISTS AND CALENDARS

Trees and Shrubs Check List	P. 135
Trees and Shrubs	P. 136
Herbs for Colorado List	P. 139
Xeriscape Garden List	P. 140
Mountain Garden List	P. 141
Patio Garden List	P. 142
Interior Garden List	P. 143
Shade Garden List	P. 144
Winter Garden List	P. 144
Rose Garden List	P. 145
Great Ornamental Grasses, Bulbs and Rock Garden Plants	P. 146
Great Ground Covers and Great Vines and Climbers	P. 147
What Blooms When Calendar	P. 148
Lawn Maintenance Calendar	P. 150
Chiles You Can Grow	P. 151
Zone Garden Map	P. 152
Index	P. 154

COLORADO GARDENING CAN BE TOUGH...

People who like to dig in the soil – and water and mix and prune and plant and weed and plan – do so for many reasons. But everyone who attempts to landscape and garden has one basic need in common – to get results.

Do you know anyone (except kids, maybe) who plays in the dirt just for fun? How about watering weeds – now that's a real good way to get rid of stress. Do you know anyone who spends hundreds of dollars on plants, seeds, trees and grass with the expectation that they will all die? The bottom line in landscaping and gardening is simple – you want to get results that you can see, feel, touch and smell.

In Colorado, you have to work at your gardening a little harder than in other parts of the country. Many would call it just plain impossible, but most people learn to accommodate themselves to the "Colorado Curses," and end up with beautiful landscapes and gardens for their efforts.

COLORADO GARDENING CURSES

Three Colorado Curses make landscaping and gardening tough. Colorado soil isn't the best. And just to make it really tough, there are several kinds of poor soil in Colorado – rocky soil, sand and clay. Some areas have all three, others have clay and the people next door have sand. Amending the soil in Colorado is the solution for this Curse. While it does take some time, there are many rewards that come from modifying the soil that Mother Nature gave to Colorado.

Colorado is dry and windy. Colorado, as a general rule, does not get a lot of moisture (an average of 13" to 18" per year). In addition, there are parts of the state that get a lot of wind. On top of both of these drying factors, Colorado has an average elevation of 6,800 feet, so the sun is very intense. Little water, wind and lots of harsh sun are not a healthy combination for flowers, trees, shrubs and grasses. What, where, when and how to plant are the solutions for this Curse.

Colorado has extreme temperature fluctuations. Some days, the temperature rises to 60°, only to drop into the high teens at night. During some weeks, you will see rain, sleet, snow and, of course, sunshine (the sun shines nearly 300 days per year). This ongoing fluctuation of temperature is hard not only on plants, but other elements in your landscape, including patios, artwork and water features. The solution for this Curse is to select the best plants and protect them, so the temperature fluctuations won't affect them as much.

COLORADO GARDENING CAN BE TOUGH…

COLORADO GARDENING BLESSINGS /

Colorado also boasts many garden blessings. Lack of moisture (and, therefore, low humidity) means we have relatively few problems with insects and diseases. All those days of sunshine bring bright, vibrant flowers. Our lawns are among the most lush and beautiful in the country. And, for some, a shorter growing season is a blessing, leaving time for other activities.

So, if you like to dig in the soil – and water and mix and prune and plant and weed and plan – and you happen to live in Colorado … you can still get results. Your success will fill your senses when you're done.

HOW TO USE MONTH-TO-MONTH GARDENING COLORADO /

Many plant labels, garden centers and catalogs refer to "zones." The U.S. Department of Agriculture Plant Hardiness Zones are a guide to tell you what plants will live in your particular area (based on average winter minimum temperatures). They also give you a good idea of when it's safe to plant to avoid frost damage. (*See page 152 for a detailed Zone Map and more information on zones.*)

Throughout the book, we use the term "higher elevations" to define those areas in Colorado that are above 6,000 feet. Generally, if you live in the higher elevations, you will want to complete the spring maintenance tips one month later and the fall maintenance tips one month earlier than people living along the Front Range and on the High Plains. There are some warmer Zone 6 pockets along the western border, and even a few Zone 7 microclimates. Spring garden maintenance in these areas would take place about one month earlier than in the rest of Colorado, and fall maintenance one month later.

FEBRUARY
/ MAINTENANCE TIPS

PERENNIALS, ANNUALS AND BULBS

☐ Check bulbs you've stored to be sure they haven't sprouted or rotted. (*See page 65.*)

☐ Order seeds and other mail-order plants, or check your local garden center for recommendations.

☐ Sow seeds indoors for petunias, dianthus, asters and marigolds (or buy transplants in May). (*See page 8.*)

☐ Test seeds saved from last year to see if they'll sprout.

Want to test seeds saved from the last gardening season? Here are some ideas...

Place about 10 seeds between sheets of damp paper towels, then seal the paper towels in a plastic food storage bag.

Keep the paper towels damp and the bag out of direct sun.

Check daily to see if seeds have sprouted. If less than half sprout, toss the bunch. Plant those that have sprouted indoors, in containers, for setting out in May!

> There are several basic rules to follow when ordering seeds or plants via mail. Make sure what you are ordering can live in your area. Ask if there will be substitutions made if a plant is out-of-stock and let them know if substitutions are acceptable. Confirm that plants were propagated in a nursery (ask where) and not dug up from some rural area of the country. Date seed packages when they arrive and keep a copy of your order form. If you want to be very sure about what you are getting, shop at your local garden center.

FEBRUARY
MAINTENANCE TIPS

TREES AND SHRUBS
☐ Gently brush the snow off trees and shrubs at higher elevations.

☐ Prune any branches that have been injured or torn by ice, snow and wind.

☐ Apply dormant oil to trees at higher elevations – this will help control aspen black spot.

☐ Thin old, overgrown deciduous shrubs (*see page 9*) before they start to bud out or bloom. (*See How-To Tip on page 119.*)

☐ Prune fruit trees late this month.

ROSES
☐ Make decisions on which roses to replace. Choose where you want to transplant or plant new roses.

Which to buy: Perennials or annuals?
Perennials provide constancy throughout the Colorado growing seasons. They can serve as backdrops for natural elements in the landscape, such as trees and shrubs, or boulders and rocks. Choose perennial plants for their variety in foliage color and texture first, then consider bloom color. This will provide an attractive display even when plants are between blooms. Add spots of annuals for the "flash" in your garden. Because of Colorado's intense sunshine, softer colors can appear washed out here, so choose annuals with more brilliant bloom colors, such as red, yellow and orange.

FEBRUARY
/ MAINTENANCE TIPS

KITCHEN GARDEN

- ☐ Sow seeds indoors for peppers, eggplant, broccoli, cabbage and tomatoes.

- ☐ Plan your kitchen garden for planting using garden center transplants available April to mid-May. (*See page 23.*)

Need a few tips on what to plant in your kitchen garden? Here are some ideas:

Check that the plants you want to grow will be ready for harvesting before the end of your growing season. Each vegetable and herb needs a specific soil temperature before it will germinate and grow.

If you live in the mountains, you can extend the growing season beyond 70 days by using plant protectors, greenhouses or cold frames.

INTERIOR GARDEN

- ☐ Thoroughly clean all indoor plants. (*See How-To Tip on page 111.*)

- ☐ Wash or replace all plant saucers to get rid of salt build-up.

> When starting plants from seeds indoors, use only clean, new, plastic pots and sterile seeding mix (potting soil). Plant the seeds at a depth of three times their width unless the seed is very small, then plant it closer to the surface. Keep the soil damp at all times, but not wet – the soil cannot dry out. Mist the seedlings as they start to grow. Some seeds need light to germinate. Most plants will germinate at a temperature of 70° to 75°, although a few like it a little colder. If you have questions, ask your local garden center.

FEBRUARY
MAINTENANCE TIPS /

GENERAL

- ☐ Prune fruit-bearing vines (especially grapes!) on a day when the temperature is above 32°. Pruning promotes bushy vines in the spring, which means more fruit.

Need help on pruning vines? Here are some ideas:

The best time to prune vines is now, when they are still dormant. If you can't do it now, wait until after they have bloomed before pruning.

Do not prune vines that grow along the ground until summer, if you want to dwarf or stunt their growth to keep them from invading trees, shrubs and flower beds.

Prune vines back by as much as one-third of their length.

- ☐ Do not add ashes from fireplaces or wood stoves to the soil around your plants – the ash can create a salt imbalance.

- ☐ Deep water trees, shrubs and roses as needed. (*See How-To Tip on page 113.*)

- ☐ Leave the compost pile alone.

It's good gardening practice to thin out old, overgrown shrubs in Colorado in late winter. This encourages the shrub to grow from the base of the plant, rather than on the existing branches, which makes for a better looking and healthier shrub. If you prune in the winter, you will have little or no shearing work (not recommended on shrubs anyway) in the spring.

FEBRUARY
MAINTENANCE TIPS

Now is a good time to replace or clean up your garden tools. Here are some ideas:

Sharp tools work better, lessen the workload and are better for the plant. Shovels, hoes, pruners, lawn mower blades and saws should have sharp, clean edges.

Safety is highly important when sharpening tools. Wear safety glasses and heavy gloves. Work in a space that is large enough to accommodate the tools you are sharpening.

A flat file or pumice stone works well on most garden tools — both can be found in hardware stores. Use the file or stone on the tool, not the tool on the sharpening device.

Sharpen away from your body, in long, rather than short, strokes. Do not go back and forth — go in one direction only.

If you are sharpening mower blades, disconnect the spark plug first. Never work on electric tools while they are plugged into the outlet.

> The truth about aspens — they are happiest at 6,500 feet or higher. If you plant them below 6,500 feet, they will require more care. Be particular about how you water them, expect problems with inkspot and leafspot diseases (more a cosmetic issue than life-threatening), oyster shell scale (must be dealt with or the tree could die) and aphids. You can expect a short life span with aspens — about 20 years — but they sucker, so this keeps them coming back without having to purchase more. Overall, while difficult to keep healthy, aspens can be a valuable addition to the landscape.

SPRING

MARCH
MAINTENANCE TIPS

_____

_____

_____

_____

_____

PERENNIALS, ANNUALS AND BULBS

☐ After removing dead blooms, fertilize bulb plants that were planted in the fall with a fertilizer slightly high in nitrogen (10-10-10).

☐ Plant perennial seeds and transplants (wait until April in the mountains).

☐ Plant pansies.

☐ Check stored bulbs (cannas, dahlias, gladiolus) for sprouting and signs of rot.

☐ Young plants may suffer when first put in the ground because of Colorado's high sun intensity, temperature fluctuations and wind. Protect them with a "row cover" available at garden centers and nurseries, or spray them with liquid seaweed or liquid potassium.

☐ In the mountains, plant vegetables and bedding plants in a greenhouse or a sunny window for planting outside in the beginning of June.

Annuals: Whether grown from seed or in the form of transplants, annuals will only live for one growing season. Then they set seed and die. Annuals are known for their vivid, bright colors. **Perennials:** These are the plants that come back every year. They often provide the "substance" in the garden, because you can count on them to grow in the same place each year. **Bulbs:** There are true bulbs, as in tulips and daffodils, then there are also rhizomes, tubers, corms and tuberous roots, as in iris, ranunculas and crocus. We use the common gardening term "bulb" to describe all of these throughout the book.

SPRING - 13

MARCH
/ MAINTENANCE TIPS

TREES AND SHRUBS

☐ Check evergreens for browning, and deciduous trees and shrubs for dead branches and buds. Remove dead wood on deciduous trees and shrubs. Prune brown branches from evergreens. (*See How-To Tip on page 119.*) Do not prune for shape at this time.

☐ Fertilize evergreens and deciduous trees and shrubs. (*See How-To Tip on page 114.*) You can fertilize in Colorado between now and July (wait until April in the mountains).

☐ Fertilize (with iron and other trace minerals) maples, wisteria, roses and other plants that tend to get yellow in mid-summer.

☐ If you didn't rake leaves or remove deciduous trees and old fruit from fruit trees in the fall, do so now.

☐ Wet snow on evergreen trees can be most damaging in spring because of its weight. Gently sweep the branches after a heavy snowfall.

☐ Prune junipers. (*See How-To Tip on page 119.*)

While leaves from healthy trees can provide a mulch, those from diseased trees can spread the disease back to the tree and other surrounding plants the next growing season. Control insects like aphids, mites and scale by raking up dead leaves from the previous season.

MARCH
MAINTENANCE TIPS

☐ Plant container and balled and burlapped trees and shrubs late this month (wait until April in the mountains). (*See How-To Tip on page 120.*)

ROSES

☐ Purchase rose bushes in containers for planting.

☐ Plant bare-root roses and transplant existing roses in late March, or as soon as the ground is workable (wait until April in the mountains). Bare-root roses need several hours water-soak before planting. (*See How-To Tip on page 118.*)

LAWN

☐ Check Lawn Maintenance Calendar. (*See page 150.*)

☐ Check lawn and garden beds for evidence of voles and treat, if necessary. (*See page 16.*)

☐ Get your lawn mower ready. Clean and sharpen blades.

☐ If there is no snow, rake and aerate bluegrass and tall fescue lawns. (It's a good idea to aerate before applying pre-emergent.)

You can buy rose bushes in containers or bare-root (usually in bags). Plant container roses after the last freeze (mid-May). Plant bare-root roses before leaves appear on the plant (can be done now or early in April). Container bushes should have three or four healthy canes that are green or red and not shriveled. Bare-root plants should have several healthy canes that are not shriveled. Check for insects and disease on top of and underneath the leaves (*see How-To Tip on page 129*). Purchase rose bushes with average to good disease resistance. Store plants in a cool (not freezing) location until planting. Container bushes should be watered periodically so the soil stays damp.

SPRING - 15

MARCH
/ MAINTENANCE TIPS

- ☐ If the spring is dry, south facing lawns may need to be watered.

- ☐ Apply a pre-emergent herbicide to your lawn if you have had crabgrass problems in the past. Do this before the crabgrass germinates in mid-April.

Have problems with crabgrass or other weeds?
Here are some ideas:

Don't scalp your lawn when mowing. Mow higher.

Don't water lightly and frequently. Water more heavily and less often.

Aerate and fertilize – thick, healthy lawns are less prone to crabgrass.

Fill in any blank spots in the lawn so crabgrass can't invade.

KITCHEN GARDEN

- ☐ Sow seeds of peas, onions, carrots, lettuce, spinach, beets, swiss chard and radishes outdoors. Plant seedlings of broccoli, cabbage, kale, brussel sprouts and cauliflower. Plant potatoes in late March.

> Voles are small rodents that look a little like mice. They eat the roots and shoots of plants in winter and the seeds and flowers in summer. You can tell you have voles if you see underground channels that raise the surface of your lawn or gardens. Remove thatch, excessive mulch, tall grass, old root vegetables and dropped fruit left over from last season. If you don't have many voles, trap them with mouse traps baited with peanut butter or apple pieces. Set the traps in the runs (dig into the channel, place the trap and put something solid on top of the hole). Gum (not mint-flavored) also may work (they can't digest it).

MARCH
MAINTENANCE TIPS

_____

_____

_____

_____

_____

_____

_____

- Plant bare-root asparagus and rhubarb.

- Plant bare-root grapes, raspberries, strawberries and fruit trees.

- Prune existing grapes, raspberries and fruit trees.

INTERIOR PLANTS

- Fertilize pots of annuals that were over-wintered indoors.

- Repot root-bound houseplants.

GENERAL

- Prepare the soil for all Colorado gardens, except those in the mountains, where you may need to wait until the ground is workable (usually April or May). (*See How-To Tip on page 127.*)

- Deep water trees, shrubs and roses as needed. (*See How-To Tip on page 113.*)

- Turn the compost pile. (*See How-To Tip on page 111.*)

If the roots of houseplants are coming out the hole in the bottom of the pot or if they are wound tightly around the inside of the pot, you need to repot the plant. You also can tell if a plant needs repotting if it grows very slowly or dries out quickly after watering. Clay or plastic pots? Use plastic – they hold moisture better but do not absorb salt from the soil. (Watering draws the salt back out of the clay pot and eventually saturates the plant, which leads to salt poisoning and death.) Use a pot only slightly larger than the last one because many plants thrive when root-bound.

APRIL
/ MAINTENANCE TIPS

PERENNIALS, ANNUALS AND BULBS

- ☐ If plants are starting to bud out, over the next month, gradually push back extra mulch that served to give plants extra protection during the winter.

- ☐ Cut back herbaceous perennials from last year (except woody perennials or evergreen perennials – plants that stay green all year). Remove plant material to the ground.

- ☐ Plant and transplant perennials on a cloudy day or in the early evening. Plant at the level of the base of the stem in well-prepared soil. (Perennials can also be planted in the mountains if the soil is workable. Transplants, not seeds, are recommended.)

Need advice on where to plant perennials?
Here are some ideas:

Find out if your plant grows better in sun or shade and plant accordingly. Perennials that like sun need about six hours of sun a day. Those that like shade should get no more than five hours of morning sun a day.

In late April, plant summer flowering bulbs such as allium, dahlias, lilies, cannas and gladiolus. (Plant gladiolus in shifts, every few weeks, so they bloom all summer.) Make sure the soil is well-prepared *(see How-To Tip on page 127)* and plant the bulb in a hole that is the same width as the bulb and three times its height. Since the growth will come out of the tip, plant with the tip facing up. Certain types of bulbs don't have a tip and they can be planted in any position (if in doubt, plant sideways). Water as needed. You can add bone meal or super-phosphate to the bottom of the hole.

APRIL
MAINTENANCE TIPS

_____

_____

_____

_____

_____

_____

_____

> The way to divide perennial plants is to dig them up in small clusters (make sure to get the roots). Thrust two gardening forks down the middle of the cluster, dividing it in two. If the cluster is very large, keep the outside growth for replanting and get rid of the inside of the plant because it is the oldest. After planting, water as needed. (*See How-To Tip on page 124.*) Perennials should be divided every three to four years.

Remember, perennials come back every year, so find out how large your plant will get and space accordingly. Lots of perennials planted close together look beautiful and are easier to weed!

Keep track of what looks good and what doesn't. You can transplant in the fall.

Soak bare-root plants in a bucket of water for about 30 minutes before planting.

☐ Plant, from seed, hardy annuals and perennials such as snapdragons, larkspur, baby's breath, bachelor's button, California poppy and pansies.

☐ Fork 2" to 3" of well-aged compost into garden beds – this will amend the soil and aerate the root area of plants.

☐ Divide fall-blooming perennial plants and bulbs in late April.

☐ Plant summer-flowering bulbs.

☐ Once the flowers on bulb plants like tulips or daffodils have died, do not prune the foliage until it has turned yellow (usually several months).

☐ Seed or overseed wildflower beds if this wasn't done last fall. (*See page 56.*)

APRIL
/ MAINTENANCE TIPS

☐ Cut back ornamental grasses at the base of the plant. (*See page 24.*)

☐ Plant ground covers.

Ground covers are plants that usually grow low to the ground and spread out.
Here are a few things to note:

Ground covers are a good substitute for lawn, though they are not meant for a lot of traffic. Once established, they require little maintenance.

Find out if your ground cover grows better in sun or shade, and plant accordingly.

Ground covers should be planted close enough to fill in fairly quickly, but not so close that they become overcrowded. The usual standard is to plant them 8" apart on center (center of plant to center of plant).

Get rid of all weeds before you plant.

TREES AND SHRUBS

☐ Continue to thin out old, overgrown shrubs by pruning no more than one-third of the oldest canes from the base. Wait to prune shrubs that are starting to bud out until after they bloom. (*See How-To Tip on page 119.*)

You can buy strawberries that are either June-bearing (a big crop once a year) or ever-bearing (the crop produces throughout the summer). Two varieties recommended for Colorado are Ogalala and Fort Laramie. Strawberries come bare-root, in containers and sometimes in transplants. Plant strawberries 18" apart in well-prepared garden soil (*see How-To Tip on page 127*), placing the base of the plant at soil level. Plants will produce more berries if they are exposed to more sunlight. To protect strawberries through the winter, mulch with 4" to 6" of straw. If you want a bigger crop, transplant the new plant that has grown at the end of each runner.

APRIL
MAINTENANCE TIPS

_____

_____

_____

_____

_____

_____

_____

To aerate the lawn, rent an aerator or hire a lawn service to remove plugs of lawn and soil. This encourages grass roots to grow deeper, which is crucial in Colorado as we do not have an overabundance of water. Do not spike the lawn because it compacts the soil around where the spike went in. When aeration is done properly, 2" or 3" deep plugs of soil are removed from the lawn. (Water the day before so that the damp (not wet) soil is more easily removed.) The holes should be approximately 2" to 3" apart. You can leave or remove the plugs. Now and in the fall are the best times to aerate lawn, not during the summer when it is hot and dry.

☐ Plant and transplant bare-root trees and shrubs. (Trees and shrubs can be planted in the mountains if the soil is workable.) (*See How-To Tip on page 120.*)

☐ Fertilize deciduous trees and shrubs (wait until May in the mountains). (*See How-To Tip on page 114.*)

☐ Push back extra mulches around shrubs.

☐ Remove tree wrap.

ROSES

☐ You can still plant or transplant bare-root rose bushes in early to mid-April, as soon as the ground is workable. (*See How-To Tip on page 118.*)

☐ Gradually remove the mound of mulch from rose bushes late in the month.

LAWN

☐ Check Lawn Maintenance Calendar. (*See page 150.*)

☐ If you haven't already done so, treat crabgrass early this month.

☐ Seed or sod cool season grasses such as bluegrass and fescues.

APRIL
/ MAINTENANCE TIPS

☐ If you have an irrigation system, test it after the winter. Make sure your system is working before you aerate and fertilize!

☐ Aerate the lawn.

☐ Fertilize the lawn (in the mountains, wait until May). (*See How-To Tip on page 114.*) After fertilizing, sweep driveway and sidewalks as fertilizer containing iron can cause spots that look like rust when you water.

KITCHEN GARDEN

☐ Continue watering "cool season" vegetables sowed in March.

☐ Hoe or hand-pull spring weeds in the vegetable garden (like dandelions).

☐ Plant strawberries. (*See page 20.*)

GENERAL

☐ Prepare the soil for all Colorado gardens, except in the mountains, where you may need to wait until the soil is workable. (*See How-To Tip on page 127.*)

☐ Begin weed control (*See How-To Tip on page 123.*)

Be cautious when planting in the mountains this month! If the winter has been somewhat mild, the soil will be workable, so trees and shrubs can be planted. Plants brought from lower elevations should still be in their dormant state or have minimal leaf expansion since low night temperatures could frost them.

MAY
MAINTENANCE TIPS /

_____

_____

_____

_____

_____

_____

- ☐ Deep water trees, shrubs and roses as needed. (*See How-To Tip on page 113.*)

- ☐ Turn compost pile. (*See How-To Tip on page 111.*)

PERENNIALS, ANNUALS AND BULBS

- ☐ Mulch around flowers and in shrub beds to conserve moisture and keep down weeds. (*See How-To Tip on page 115.*)

- ☐ Plant annuals at the same depth as in the container (or slightly higher in very clay soil) in soil-amended beds. (*See How-To Tip on page 127.*)

- ☐ Sow annual flower seeds, such as cosmos and zinnias. (Be patient – planting from seed will take longer than buying and planting transplants.)

- ☐ Set out any plants sowed from seeds indoors.

- ☐ Check plants for aphids and treat if necessary. (*See How-To Tip on page 129.*)

- ☐ Pinch mums so they are bushy in the fall. (*See How-To Tip on page 112.*)

When you buy plants for your garden (flower or vegetable), look for six-packs of seedlings that are not dried out or soaking wet, not wilted-looking or yellow and not spindly. The plant should be one-third soil depth to no more than two-thirds plant foliage. Look for plants with lots of buds and a few flowers (to give you an idea of color). Look for plants with healthy, compact foliage.

MAY
/ MAINTENANCE TIPS

☐ After mid-May, put out annuals and perennials that have been overwintered indoors in pots.

☐ Plant containers and windowboxes with herbs and annuals. Use good potting soil and water every other day (every day during the summer).

☐ Rake 2" to 3" of compost into all garden areas and beds in the mountains.

☐ Plant ornamental grasses.

☐ Mow (at highest setting) or prune established ground covers to clean them up and remove winterburn.

TREES AND SHRUBS

☐ If you shear your hedges (not usually recommended in Colorado because it's hard on the plant) never take off more than one-third of the growth. The top should narrower than the base so the sun reaches all areas.

☐ Deadhead lilacs after they finish blooming. (*See How-To Tip on page 112.*)

> When ornamental grass is cut back, the plant loses some nutrients. Apply an organic or inorganic fertilizer (label should read 1-2-1 or something close) at the rate of one to two pounds per 100 square feet. Ornamental grasses should be planted just as you would a rose bush, with the top of the root ball slightly below the ground. They can be planted from now until the end of the growing season in September. Do not transplant ornamental grasses after mid-July. If the container is two gallons (#2) or larger, plant the grass as you would a shrub. (*See How-To Tip on page 120.*) If smaller than two gallons, plant as you would a perennial.

MAY
MAINTENANCE TIPS

_____

_____

_____

_____

_____

_____

- ☐ Using a hand pruner, clip off new candles on evergreens to maintain compact growth. (*See How-To Tip on page 119.*)

- ☐ Mulch around trees and shrubs. (*See How-To Tip on page 115.*)

- ☐ Deep water trees, shrubs and roses in the mountains. (*See How-To Tip on page 113.*)

ROSES

- ☐ Fertilize your rose bushes. (*See How-To Tip on page 114.*)

- ☐ Prune back rose bushes and remove mounding that remains.

- ☐ Plant container roses after the last frost. (*See How-To Tip on page 118.*)

LAWN

- ☐ Check the Lawn Maintenance Calendar. (*See page 150.*)

- ☐ Seed or sod cool season grasses like bluegrass and fescues.

- ☐ Seed any dead areas in your lawn caused by disease or insects. (*See page 54.*)

> When planting annuals, dig individual holes for plants in amended soil (*See How-To Tip on page 127*). Pinch off any blooms and make sure the plant and roots are wet. Remove the container and plant in heavy clay soil in a hole at the same depth as it was in the container, or slightly higher. Disrupt the roots to stimulate and encourage them to grow out instead of circling in the ground. The label or seed package should state the type of location the plant needs (sun, shade, partial sun/shade) and how far apart to plant. Soak the ground around the plant thoroughly and mulch. (*See How-To Tip on page 115.*) The best time to plant is on a cool day or early in the morning or evening.

SPRING - 25

MAY
/ MAINTENANCE TIPS

- ☐ Mow lawn to no less than 2" and never cut any more than one-third of the growth in a single cutting.

- ☐ If needed, apply broadleaf weed killer on the lawn with a drop spreader or spot spray it on.

- ☐ Apply lawn fertilizer in the mountains.

KITCHEN GARDEN

- ☐ Plant a salsa garden.

A salsa garden is easy to grow. Here are some ideas:

The plants in a typical salsa garden are chile peppers (your choice for flavor and heat) (*see page 151*), roma tomatoes, onions, garlic, tomatillos, cilantro, basil, Mexican oregano and parsley.

Grow all the ingredients and make your own combinations of salsas.

As a general rule, for every jalapeño or chile plant you will need one tomato plant.

You can serve your salsa fresh, or freeze or can it.

- ☐ Purchase vegetable transplants and seeds for direct sowing.

Cool season grasses, such as bluegrass and fescues, perform best during cool (not cold) months of the spring and fall. Warm season grasses, such as buffalograss and blue gramma, grow best during the warmer months. Water cool season grasses less in the spring and fall, and more in the hot summer months, so they'll stay green. While it takes longer for the warm season grasses to turn green, they require much less water than the cool season grasses to stay green during the hottest months of the year. Rake the area smooth and either sod or seed. If you sod, be sure to amend the soil first.

MAY
MAINTENANCE TIPS /

_____

_____

_____

_____

_____

_____

_____

Have problems with rabbits? Here are some ideas:

Surround the garden or individual plant with chicken wire, leaving no openings. Bury the wire at least 4" into the soil.

Apply blood meal around the base of the plant. (Repeat after watering.)

Make a mixture of cayenne pepper (a little goes a long way) and water, and spray on the plants. (This remedy needs to be repeated, especially if it snows or rains.)

☐ Plant radishes, cucumbers, zucchini and beans from seed. Reseed beans every few weeks to extend their harvest.

☐ If you want pumpkins by Halloween, plant the seeds now.

☐ Plant tomatoes and peppers from transplants at the end of the month.

☐ From transplants, plant herbs such as basil, parsley and chives. Try growing basil and dill from seed.

☐ From transplants, plant flowers like marigolds, nasturtiums and pansies in the paths, between rows and around the perimeter of the kitchen garden.

Here's a vote for planting zinnias from seed. Zinnias will grow in average soil. They don't need lots of water. They come in all sizes and about six colors. They like the sun and areas with good air circulation. They will bloom from early summer to late September. Zinnias are, in short, a flower made for our area. Water zinnias at the base of the plant, not overhead, to decrease the chances for powdery mildew. (Don't plant the larger, later-blooming varieties at higher elevations because they flower too late in the season.)

MAY
/ MAINTENANCE TIPS

Want to keep your kitchen garden free of diseases, pests and weeds? Here are some ideas:

Select healthy transplants that are stocky and have not flowered or set fruit.

Interplant flowers and herbs throughout a kitchen garden to help distract and confuse insect pests throughout the summer.

Mulch garden pathways with old newspapers covered with straw or grass clippings. DO NOT use clippings treated with herbicides. Because newspaper might leach aluminum, use only a thin layer and keep it away from edible plants.

Don't over-crowd your plants – air circulation is important and disease is less likely to spread.

If you keep your garden clean, you can help minimize disease. Immediately throw away diseased plants and old, unpicked vegetables. Don't add diseased material to the compost pile.

If you're interested in preserving your extra fruit or vegetables (freezing, canning or drying), contact your county extension office for information.

If you are growing tomatoes for the first time, start by purchasing the more common varieties found in garden centers – Early Girl, Better Boy, Celebrity and Fantastic. Harden off the plants for a few days on a porch or protected area outside, then plant in prepared soil in the full sun. Plant up to the first set of leaves. Follow the tag for spacing between plants. Place extra-large cages around the tomatoes after the second week (the tomatoes will eventually grow into them). Tomatoes need consistently warm weather and plenty of water (the soil must be kept evenly moist to produce the best fruit).

MAY
MAINTENANCE TIPS /

- Begin harvesting spring-planted cool season vegetables like peas, lettuce, spinach and broccoli. (*See How-To Tip on page 116.*)

INTERIOR PLANTS

- This is a good month to divide and take cuttings from interior plants.

- Repot, in new potting soil, poinsettias that you plan to set outdoors in July. After repotting, cut the stems back to within 4" of the soil.

GENERAL

- Plant climbing vines in the early part of this month for great results the rest of the summer.

- Many utilities, such as gas, telephone, electric and cable lines, are buried on your property. To avoid costly and potentially deadly consequences, always call the Utility Notification Center of Colorado (800-922-1987) before digging trenches or holes. They will come and mark the locations of the utility lines for you.

- Replenish organic mulches. (*See How-To Tip on page 115.*)

There are some varieties of climbing vines that grow well in Colorado: Virginia creeper, silverlace, English ivy, clematis, honeysuckle, woodbine, Boston ivy, grape and hop. Trellis climbing vines for show, easier maintenance and to keep them from crowding out other plants, trees and shrubs. Allow for airflow on trellises near buildings, especially if on the hot south or west exposures. (Do not allow vines to climb the sides of wood houses or fences because they can cause wood rot.)

MAY
MAINTENANCE TIPS

☐ Continue to weed your garden before weeds get too big or too numerous. (*See How-To Tip on page 123.*)

☐ Keep small stones swept off patios and walkways for safety reasons.

☐ Water your plants, trees, shrubs and lawn infrequently, but thoroughly. (*See How-To Tip on page 124.*)

☐ Turn the compost pile. (*See How-To Tip on page 111.*)

Frustrated with insect problems in your garden? Here are some ideas:

Ladybugs and lacewings both serve as natural predators against a variety of harmful insects in the garden. You can buy the larvae of both at a local garden center or you can check the Internet for sources.

Plants such as carrots, mints and daisies all attract beneficial insects to your garden.

Control aphids by getting rid of any ants.

Try a strong stream of water to get rid of harmful insects on your plants. If that doesn't work, you can pick the larger pests off by hand (*or see How-To section on page 129*).

Rock gardens often look their best when displayed on a "berm." A berm is a raised area created by the mounding of fill dirt and smooth grading prior to soil preparation, boulder placement and planting. If you have a flat landscape and don't want to put in a berm, large rocks, when grouped and set into the ground, will give the illusion of a raised area. For the most natural look, use rocks that come from your geographic area. If you bring in boulders, they should be buried to one-third their size into the grade. Otherwise, they will look unnatural. Generally, rock gardens do best in sunny areas.

SUMMER

JUNE
MAINTENANCE TIPS

_____

_____

_____

_____

_____

_____

PERENNIALS, ANNUALS AND BULBS

- ☐ Deadhead flowers as they fade to promote continuous bloom. (*See How-To Tip on page 112.*)

- ☐ Continue to plant summer flowering bulbs, like cannas, dahlias and gladiolus. (Plant a few gladiolus each week to have continuous blooms throughout the summer.)

- ☐ Note places in your landscape that could be filled next year with spring bulbs. Plant in the fall.

- ☐ Divide spring bulbs as the foliage dies. (*See box this page.*)

- ☐ Fertilize annuals and perennials with nitrogen-based fertilizer.

- ☐ In early June, continue planting herbs and annuals in containers for your porches, window boxes, patios and decks.

- ☐ Plant annuals in containers and set in bare spots in your landscape. (There may be some good bargains on annuals now.)

If you don't divide bulbs like tulips, crocus and hyacinths every three to five years, they will crowd each other out. Overcrowding with some bulbs can result in very small flowers. Other bulbs, like daffodils, actually tend to get bigger and better each year. Only divide them if they are getting overcrowded. Dig up a clump of the bulbs just after the foliage of the plant starts to turn yellow. (Make sure you dig deep enough to get the roots.) Then break off the bulbs from one another and either replant or store in a dry place until the fall. Do not cut off the foliage from the bulb even after you've divided them.

JUNE
/ MAINTENANCE TIPS

Want to brighten up your landscape? Annuals planted in containers and set into or planted directly into your garden will do the job. Here are some ideas:

Find out how much sun your annuals need before you decide where to plant them. If you put shade-loving annuals in a sunny area the plants will suffer!

Decide what height you will need before you plant your containers. You may need plants that add height for the back of a garden, or some that are shorter for the front edge of a border.

Plant annuals using good potting soil, in containers that drain well.

Most annuals must be pinched back to stay looking good all summer. (*See How-To Tip on page 112.*)

Here are some annuals you might not have thought of: coleus (provides beautiful texture and color), flowering tobacco (great scent and comes in a variety of heights and colors), gazania (drought-tolerant flowers), heliotrope (very Victorian with a nice scent and clustered flowers) and cleome (showy and tall).

Geraniums can be overwintered and then set outside for summer enjoyment. They tend to grow long, sparse stems if they are not cut back periodically. With pruners, cut stems about 2" to 3" from where they connect to another stem. To propagate new transplants, leave the tip of the stem and cut down about 5", just below one of the lines running around the stem. Dip the cut end into a rooting hormone for a few minutes. Plant the cuttings about 1½" deep and the width of the cut stems. Keep the soil moist until they root. (The transplants can be moved outdoors but don't move the "mother" plant outside for a few weeks.)

JUNE
MAINTENANCE TIPS

_____

_____

_____

_____

_____

_____

There are many creative ways to plant containers for your porch, deck, patio or window box. Seed an annual grass for a nice base for the flowers (don't overdo the amount). Lettuce makes a great filler plant. Plant strawberries in hanging baskets. In large containers, plant a miniature rock garden with rocks of different shapes and sizes, and plants like dianthus, allium, campanula and sedum. Or, grow water lilies and Japanese iris in an old, lined wooden trough or half-barrel. A combination of pansies, peppermint and golden sage looks great. Surround small chile pepper plants with oregano or sage. If your need more ideas, see what your local garden center has done!

TREES AND SHRUBS

☐ Make sure trees and shrubs are getting enough water.

ROSES

☐ Fertilize rose bushes after the first round of flowers has started to die. (*See How-To Tip on page 114.*)

☐ Cut back suckers from rose bushes. (*See page 36.*)

☐ If the spring has been a wet one, watch for black spot and powdery mildew. (*See How-To Tip on page 129.*)

LAWN

☐ Check the Lawn Maintenance Calendar. (*See page 150.*)

☐ Check drip and lawn system. Remove any emitters that are clogged or overwatering and add emitters to areas where the soil is dry. (*See How-To Tip on page 124.*)

☐ Seed or sod warm season grasses like blue gramma and buffalograss.

☐ Mow lawn to no less than 2" and never cut any more than one-third of the growth in a single cutting.

☐ Watch lawns on south and west faces for drought stress.

JUNE
MAINTENANCE TIPS

KITCHEN GARDEN

- Water seeds and transplants daily after planting. Do this for two weeks to keep the soil moist and allow seeds to germinate.

- Shade new transplants between 10 a.m. and 4 p.m. the first week they are planted if daytime temperatures exceed 92°. Gradually introduce the plants to the sun.

- Finish harvesting spring-planted cool season vegetables such as peas, lettuce and spinach.

- Look for radishes planted in May to be ready toward the end of this month.

- It's not too late to plant many vegetables, especially at lower elevations. Check the number of growing days for particular varieties.

- Watch for caterpillars on crops and treat with Bt (*see page 129*) or pick them off, then cover plants with row covers.

- Plant vegetable gardens and bedding plants early this month at higher elevations.

> If you have a rose bush that now produces some roses that are different than what they were originally, check the bush carefully. If it still has any branches growing from the graft, the bush will continue to grow as the original if you remove the suckers with the different roses below the graft. If all the suckers are growing from the roots or below the graft, the bush will not grow the original roses again. (To avoid this problem, ask at your garden center for roses grown on their own roots.)

JUNE
MAINTENANCE TIPS

_____
_____
_____
_____
_____
_____
_____

INTERIOR PLANTS

☐ Thoroughly clean all indoor plants. (*See How-To Tip on page 111.*)

☐ Wash out or replace all plant saucers to get rid of salt build-up.

GENERAL

☐ Check for diseases or insects that may be attacking plants. (*See How-To Tip on page 129.*)

☐ Weed your garden once a week. (*See How-To Tip on page 123.*) Stop using herbicides on weeds at this time and remove weeds with a hoe or by hand. (Many herbicides, when used to control weeds in hot summer weather, can cause injury to nearby healthy plants.)

☐ Keep small stones swept off patios and walkways for safety reasons.

☐ This month can be very hot and windy with high light intensity. Check for extra water needs and plant protection. (*See How-To Tips on pages 115 and 124.*)

☐ Turn the compost pile once every two weeks during this month. (*See How-To Tip on page 111.*)

This is a good time to assess how much water your gardens are getting. Remember, garden beds need, on average, 2" of water per week, and it's preferable to water deeply and less frequently. (Lawns need about 1" of water per week, on average.) Set margarine cups out in 5 or 6 areas of your garden beds. Measure and mark ½" and 1" from the bottom on the cup's side. Start your water source (irrigation system, drip emitters, sprinkler) and check the cups in 20 minutes. You will then be able to tell how long you need to water each area each week. You can also see which areas are getting too much water and which are not getting enough.

SUMMER - 37

JULY
MAINTENANCE TIPS

PERENNIALS, ANNUALS AND BULBS

☐ Continue to pinch, cut and deadhead perennials and annuals.

☐ For better fall flowers, pinch mums only until the end of the month, then stop.

☐ Divide and replant Oriental poppies after the foliage begins to die.

☐ Create an environment with plants that will attract hummingbirds.

☐ Create an environment with plants that will attract butterflies. (*See page 39.*)

Want to build a home for butterflies?
Here are a few ideas:

Because it can get windy, plant your butterfly garden in a sheltered or enclosed area. Trees and shrubs work, as do fences or a trellis with a flowering vine.

Butterflies will perch in shrubs, tree crevices, under bark or in log piles.

Because butterflies like heat, having rocks and evergreens in your garden will help attract them (rocks and evergreens absorb the sun.)

If you want to attract hummingbirds to your garden, remember that they like sunny areas, red or orange objects and shapes that are tubular (for their long, tube-like tongue). Because they need to see the plants from a long distance (at least 30 feet overhead), colors should be vivid enough to catch their attention. If you want to attract both butterflies and hummingbirds, plant separate gardens so they don't compete with one another. Some of the plants hummingbirds like best are flowering crabapple trees, clematis, verbena, geraniums, bee balm, phlox, sweet William, coral bells, morning glories, gladiolus and dianthus.

JULY
MAINTENANCE TIPS

_____

_____

_____

_____

_____

_____

_____

> If you want to attract butterflies to your garden, remember that they like bright, damp areas with flat stones or boards where they can sun themselves. You first must create a healthy environment for the butterfly caterpillar, then one that attracts the adult butterfly. Plants necessary for butterfly caterpillars are wild lupine, goldenrod, wild asters, statice, parsley and dill. (They also like milkweed, thistle, clover, etc., but these weeds aren't always compatible with other garden goals.) Some plants butterflies like best are petunia, marigold, foxglove, impatiens, cosmos, verbena, bee balm, snapdragon, daylily, strawberry, black-eyed Susan, coreopsis and liatris.

Fill a container with sand and saturate it with water. (Butterflies can't drink from open water.)

☐ Watch for tobacco budworm, which feeds on flower buds of petunias, geraniums and flowering tobacco. Pick off or treat these tiny caterpillars with Bt (*see page 129*) as soon as you find them.

TREES AND SHRUBS

☐ Do not use high nitrogen fertilizer on trees from now until next March.

☐ Make sure trees and shrubs are getting enough water during the hottest months. (*See How-To Tip on page 124.*)

☐ To produce larger fruit, thin the tiny fruits on your trees to a hand-span between each.

☐ Watch for insect outbreaks on newly planted trees.

ROSES

☐ Keep an eye on rose leaves for black spot and powdery mildew. Treat if necessary. (*See How-To Tip on page 129.*)

JULY
MAINTENANCE TIPS

- Deadhead roses after they bloom. (*See How-To Tip on page 112.*)

- Fertilize roses. (*See How-To Tip on page 114.*)

LAWN

- Check Lawn Maintenance Calendar. (*See page 150.*)

- Non-treated grass makes a good mulch around plants and in vegetable garden pathways.

- Avoid fertilizer that is high in nitrogen when temperatures are hot. (You can use slow-release nitrogen.)

- Mow the lawn to no less than 2" in height, never cutting more than one-third of the growth in a single mowing.

- Resharpen lawn mower blades.

- Hot, south-facing lawns need extra water because they dry out quickly in summer.

- Lawns with excessive thatch (greater than ½") may need extra water.

- During the hottest parts of the summer, lawns should get about 2" of water per week instead of the normal 1" per week at other times.

_____
_____
_____
_____
_____
_____
_____

Too much thatch in your lawn isn't healthy because it prevents movement of air and water to the root zone of your grass. Thatch is a spongy, organic layer composed of grass roots, stems and other dark organic materials. When you have a lot of thatch, grass roots will grow in the thatch, not the soil. Because thatch doesn't hold water, the lawn can dry out more easily than normal, especially in cold weather or hot temperatures. If your lawn has a lot of thatch, water more thoroughly and aerate (preferably in the fall or spring months).

JULY
MAINTENANCE TIPS

_____

_____

_____

_____

_____

_____

KITCHEN GARDEN

☐ Make sure the garden is well-mulched to protect plants during the heat of the day. Keep heat-loving weeds under control. *(See How-To Tip on page 123.)*

☐ Begin harvesting the first tomatoes around mid-July.

☐ Begin harvesting cool season vegetables and herbs in the higher elevations. *(See How-To Tip on page 116.)*

☐ Pull spring-planted cool season vegetables that are finished producing. Add the plants to the compost pile.

☐ Many cool season vegetables can be planted this month for fall harvesting. Peas, cabbage and lettuce are not only frost-tolerant, but their flavor actually improves after a light frost. *(See page 116.)*

☐ Watch for grasshoppers if the weather has been hot and dry.

☐ Watch for slugs and snails if the weather has been cooler and wet. *(See How-To Tip on page 129.)*

There are a number of flowers you can grow that are good to eat. (Usually it's the petals you eat, not the stems or the centers.) When you cook with edible flowers, use only petals that you know are home-grown and haven't been treated with chemicals. There are a number of ways to prepare petals – dip in batter and deep fry, add to soups and salads, steam in stir fry, stuff and bake, use to make tea or add as a garnish. For sweet eating, make candied flowers. Some more common edible flowers include squash and pumpkin blossoms, roses, daylilies, tulips, pansies, borage, nasturtiums, dianthus, scented geraniums and chrysanthemums.

JULY
MAINTENANCE TIPS

INTERIOR PLANTS

☐ Poinsettias that still have their leaves can be set outside.

Poinsettias are nice additions to the summer garden. Here are a few tips:

Help your poinsettia acclimate to the outdoors by putting it in a shady area, like a porch, for a week or so.

It is recommended that you leave the poinsettia in the pot when you move it outdoors. Either plant the pot or set the poinsettia in and among other plants and flowers in your garden.

Place or plant the pot in a lightly shaded area.

Water so that the soil in the pot is moist, but not soggy.

Remove 1" from each stem in August, so the plant stays short and stocky.

☐ Keep houseplants out of the direct sun to protect tender leaves from burning.

GENERAL

☐ Spider mites really begin to emerge this month, so keep in touch with your plants, trees and shrubs, and treat when necessary. (*See How-To Tip on page 129.*)

There are several ways to help cut flowers last longer. First, cut flowers before mid-morning. The stems should be cut at an angle and immediately put into a bucket of water. Use sharp shears. Once inside, do your trim work with the stems under water. The stems of roses and poppies should be plunged into boiling water first and then transferred into the vase or container. Get rid of any leaves that will be submerged. If you add floral food, you only need to change the water every two days. If not, change the water daily and keep cutting 1/2" from the stems each time you change the water. Don't place the arrangement in or very near the sun or in warm areas.

JULY
MAINTENANCE TIPS

_____

_____

_____

_____

_____

_____

_____

☐ If you cut woody-stemmed branches (such as forsythia or lilacs) to put in an arrangement, hit several inches of the bottoms of the stems with a hammer before putting in water.

☐ Continue to weed your garden. (*See How-To Tip on page 123.*) Watch to see that weeds don't grow so large that they flower and drop seeds. (This creates more weeds!)

☐ Keep up with watering needs in your garden. Although we can get frequent afternoon showers, the amount of moisture can be deceiving – these storms rarely produce enough water to soak the soil and benefit your plants. (*See How-To Tip on page 124.*)

☐ Keep small stones swept off patios and walkways for safety reasons.

☐ Turn the compost pile twice this month. (*See How-To Tip on page 111.*)

Spider mites like our hot, dry weather in June, July, August and part of September. A possible sign of spider mites is fine webbing on plants. The leaves or needles on evergreen trees will turn dull green/yellow and appear speckled. Red "speckles" may move on the underside of leaves. You want to treat spider mites because they can go dormant during cold weather, only to return when it gets warm again. Lacewings are the natural enemy of spider mites. If you haven't seen many lacewings in your garden, ask your garden center if they sell lacewing eggs or larvae, or check the Internet for sources. If lacewings don't do the job, look for other remedies on page 129.

AUGUST
MAINTENANCE TIPS

PERENNIALS, ANNUALS AND BULBS

- ☐ Continue to deadhead, pinch and cut annuals and perennials. (*See How-To Tip on page 112.*)

- ☐ Pinch back spindly annuals and fertilize for another spurt of growth. (*See page 45.*)

- ☐ Divide bearded iris bulbs in early August.

- ☐ Select and cut flowers, grasses and leaves that you want to dry for display in arrangements.

TREES AND SHRUBS

- ☐ Remove dead or diseased evergreen branches. (*See How-To Tip on page 119.*)

- ☐ Do not fertilize trees and shrubs until next spring.

- ☐ Make sure trees and shrubs are getting enough water during August.

ROSES

- ☐ Last month to fertilize rose bushes. Do not fertilize after the middle of the month.

- ☐ Stop deadheading roses so they can begin to harden off and form rose hips.

> The feel and colors of spring, summer and fall can all be kept alive by drying your favorite flowers, grasses and leaves. Gather the stems together and secure them with a rubber band. Hang upside down in a warm, dark area until the stems become brittle. Store the finished dried plants in paper bags.

AUGUST
MAINTENANCE TIPS

_____

_____

_____

_____

_____

_____

> Annuals tend to have a pause in growth in August. To pep them up, cut the stems back by at least half, use an organic fertilizer in the soil around them and soak the plant and soil thoroughly. You can also fertilize with a 5-10-5 fertilizer or a water soluble fertilizer.

☐ Watch for powdery mildew on roses, flowers and squash. Water early in the day to help prevent mildew.

LAWN

☐ Check Lawn Maintenance Calendar. (*See page 150.*)

☐ For lower elevations, this is the last month you can install warm season grasses.

☐ Mow lawn to no less than 2½" and never cut more than one-third of the growth.

☐ Pay particular attention to good watering practices this month. Stressed areas in full sun or on southern or western slopes may need extra watering.

KITCHEN GARDEN

☐ Continue harvesting tomatoes, warm season vegetables and herbs. (*See How-To Tip on page 116.*)

Want to use the herbs you grow as seasonings in your food? Here are some ideas:

Basil tastes good in tomatoes, herb oil, vinaigrettes, Italian dishes, egg and cheese dishes, and with rosemary in bread.

AUGUST
MAINTENANCE TIPS

Chives can be used with sour cream for a dip, in egg or potato dishes, in vegetable seasonings and in Mexican dishes.

Dill is great in salads, dips and dressings, with fish, on tomatoes, and in egg or chicken dishes.

Mint is good in tea, lemonade and other fresh drinks.

Oregano is good in stews, soups and Italian dishes.

Parsley is a good garnish and can also be used in almost any main course, salad or soup. It's also good in egg and cheese dishes.

Rosemary can be used in breads, in vinaigrettes and in chicken and pork dishes.

Sage is good in Italian dishes, stuffing and vegetable seasonings.

Thyme can be used on vegetables and tomatoes, in turkey stuffing and in stews.

☐ Begin to harvest beans, peppers and cucumbers. (*See How-To Tip on page 116.*)

☐ Harvest garlic in lower elevations.

☐ Plants used to make salsa may be ready for harvest. (*See How-To tip on page 116.*)

> **What to do with all those chile peppers you've grown? Make a ristra! Ristras are the long, hanging decorations made from chile peppers. Pick the chile pods when they are red or starting to turn red (usually this month). To make a 3-foot-long ristra, you will need about ¾ of a bushel of chile peppers. Tie three chile peppers together by wrapping cotton string around the stems. Then tie the group to a piece of twine. Repeat with sets of three chile peppers, tying the groups onto the main piece of twine 3" to 4" apart. At the top of the twine, tie a piece of looped wire so you can hang the ristra. Hang the ristra outside in a cool, dry, airy place until it is completely dry.**

AUGUST
MAINTENANCE TIPS

_____

_____

_____

_____

_____

_____

☐ Plant cool season vegetables now for fall harvesting. (*See page 116.*)

☐ Make certain plants are watered adequately on hot August days.

☐ Watch for pests like cabbage butterflies and tomato hornworms. (*See page 48.*)

☐ Watch for spider mites on tomatoes and peppers. Hose off with insecticidal soap in early morning. (*See How-To Tip on page 129.*)

☐ Share extra produce with your local food bank.

☐ Zucchini puree is great for the compost pile, when friends and neighbors no longer want any more of your zucchini.

GENERAL
☐ Create a garden "junkyard."

Every garden has plants that just don't seem to perform or do well, regardless of your best efforts. Instead of waiting until a plant dies, try transplanting it into your "junkyard," the "I don't know what else to do with it" catch-all garden.
Here are some ideas:

Plan your junkyard for an area that isn't seen by others – don't put it in front of your house!

After mid-August, do not fertilize woody, flowering shrubs like rose bushes. You don't want to continue to stimulate more growth than necessary. This way, the shrubs will be encouraged to harden off before the first freeze.

AUGUST
MAINTENANCE TIPS

Take special care to amend the soil properly (*see How-To Tip on page 127*) and to make sure the garden has a good source for water. (Since this garden is a last-ditch effort, you might as well give the plants the best chance possible!)

Throughout the growing season, note which plants are not doing well. Move them quickly into the junkyard.

Make sure that the problem with the plant isn't insects or disease. (If this is what you suspect, treat the plant, don't move it.) (*See How-To Tip on page 129.*)

You can put more than plants in your junkyard. How about broken pottery to form a pathway? Or old furniture planted over with vines?

☐ Pay special attention to insect and disease problems this month.

☐ Weed your garden frequently.

☐ Make sure plants in the garden are getting adequate water this month.

☐ Start a compost pile with leftovers from the garden. (*See How-To Tip on page 111.*)

Tomato hornworms are green caterpillars that are 3 to 5 inches long and have black horns on their rear ends. Left unchecked, they can do severe damage to tomato plants. The easiest remedy is to pick them off by hand. Spraying with Bt (Bacillus thuringiensis) is usually effective and is safe to use on edible plants. If you see white cocoons on the back of the hornworm, leave them alone because these hold parasitic wasps (the natural enemy of the hornworm) who are doing their job. Another suggestion is to plant tomatoes in plastic containers because pests like the hornworm can't easily climb the slick sides of the pot.

FALL

SEPTEMBER
MAINTENANCE TIPS

_____

_____

_____

_____

_____

_____

_____

There are a number of bulbs you can buy to plant in the fall for spring blooming: daffodils, tulips (hybrid tulips will die out after a few seasons), lilies, snowdrops, crocus and hyacinth. All of these fall bulbs can be left in the ground for years. They do not need to be dug up in fall, unlike bulbs planted in spring that bloom in summer. They should, however, be divided periodically. (*See page 33.*) When you buy bulbs, buy them big, regardless of the type. If the bulbs are slightly mushy, soft or dried up, don't buy them. If they look damaged, don't buy them. Buying bulbs on sale might be risky, especially if they're small.

PERENNIALS, ANNUALS AND BULBS

☐ Choose any annuals you want to overwinter and pot them now. At higher elevations, bring inside before a frost and set near a sunny window or in a greenhouse. Be sure to disinfect any of the plants before you bring them inside. (*See page 76.*)

☐ Transplant and/or divide peonies if necessary. (Caution: peonies hate to be moved!) (*See page 52.*)

☐ Transplant and/or divide spring and summer-blooming perennials (but not fall perennials). (*See page 19.*)

☐ Plant new perennials.

☐ Plant pansies, violas and mums for fall color.

☐ Sow seed for self-seeding annuals like California poppies, love-in-a-mist and cosmos.

☐ Divide daylilies now. (*See page 19.*)

☐ Plant ground covers.

☐ Plant ornamental grasses. (*See page 146 for a list.*)

SEPTEMBER
/ MAINTENANCE TIPS

☐ Purchase bulbs for fall planting (You can buy from garden centers or mail order catalogs.) *(See page 51.)* Wait until October to plant.

☐ Collect and save seeds from your flowers and vegetables to plant in your garden next year.

How do you collect seeds from your favorite plants? Here are some ideas:

Mark the plants that you want to gather seed from so you don't accidentally pick all the blooms. You'll know when the pods are ready because they will become dry but won't have opened and scattered their seed. (Rarely do all the pods on one plant open at the same time, so even if the first few pods open, you'll still be able to gather plenty.)

If the pod is fragile, cover it with a paper bag (tie it at the bottom of the pod) before it gets dry.

After you have gathered the seeds from the pods, air dry them for a week. Store them in airtight containers in a cool, dry place. (Mark the containers with the names of the plants.)

☐ Fall cleanup takes place in the higher elevations this month. Cut down all dry perennials and water them thoroughly. Compost or discard all annuals and bedding plants.

> To transplant and/or divide peonies, dig up the entire plant, making sure to get all the roots. At the crown of each plant, there will be pink buds. Use a knife to divide the plant so there are no more than three buds in each division. Dig a hole in amended soil (*see How-To Tip on page 127*) and plant your divided peonies close to the surface, covering the buds with only 1" of soil. Water well after transplanting. Peonies like sunny locations that drain well.

SEPTEMBER
MAINTENANCE TIPS

_____

_____

_____

_____

_____

_____

TREES AND SHRUBS

☐ Plant or transplant evergreens from one location in the garden to another before the weather turns cool. (*See How-To Tip on page 120.*)

☐ Harvest pears before they ripen on the tree – pears picked green have better flavor.

☐ Do not fertilize trees and shrubs now.

ROSES

☐ Stop deadheading and let rose hips form. The rose plant will now begin to harden off for the winter.

LAWN

☐ Check Lawn Maintenance Calendar. (*See page 150.*)

☐ Mow lawn to 2". Never cut more than one-third of the growth in a single cutting.

☐ Reseed parts of lawn that need it. (*See page 54.*)

☐ Winterize irrigation systems in higher elevations. (*See page 58.*)

☐ At higher elevations, apply winterizer fertilizer on the lawn and aerate.

☐ Install cool season grasses.

This month is a good time to remove grass that grows right up to the trunks of trees. Dig out the grass (or use glyphosate, but don't get any on the tree or tree suckers). Once the grass is dead, put down mulch, such as wood chips, where the grass has been removed. This needs to be done so that when mowers or weed-eaters are used, the tree trunk isn't damaged. (If you keep hitting the trunk with lawn equipment, the tree may eventually die.)

SEPTEMBER
/ MAINTENANCE TIPS

KITCHEN GARDEN

- ☐ Continue harvesting cucumbers, beans, zucchini and other vegetables from the garden. (*See How-To Tip on page 116.*)

- ☐ Harvest all green tomatoes before the first frost. They will turn red after removal from the plants. (*See How-To Tip on page 116.*)

- ☐ Harvest cabbage, carrots and brussel sprouts after the first mild frost (32°). (*See How-To Tip on page 116.*)

- ☐ Harvest garlic. Save some of the ripest cloves for replanting in October. (*See How-To Tip on page 116.*)

- ☐ Harvest and dry herbs.

If you don't plan to have an inside herb garden during the winter, dry those from your garden to use until next spring. Here are some ideas:

Cut the herbs in the mid-morning to help preserve the flavors in the herbs. Trim off up to one-third of the plant to use for drying. Wait to chop herbs until after they are dried.

Spring and summer activities can be hard on lawns. Bare spots caused by disease, insects, dogs, kids and mower scalping can be corrected by reseeding. With a garden fork, stab the soil in the bare spot and then rake the area. Spread the seed by hand (not on a windy day!), using one ounce per square yard of the same seed as the rest of your lawn. Lightly cover the seed with amended soil from another part of the yard and use a hoe to lightly compress the soil (don't totally bury the seed). Water with a fine spray and keep the soil damp (not wet) until germination, which should occur in one to two weeks. Then water on the same schedule as the rest of the lawn.

SEPTEMBER
MAINTENANCE TIPS

_____

_____

_____

_____

_____

_____

_____

When air-drying, tie the herbs together in bundles, put in a paper bag that has holes punched in the sides, put a rubber band around the top and hang upside down. For best results, dry indoors.

You can also dry herbs in a cool oven by layering the leaves (not touching) between layers of paper towels. The light in the oven should be enough to dry the herbs out overnight.

Store herbs in airtight containers away from heat and away from light. (Don't store them above or near the oven or stove.)

INTERIOR PLANTS

- ☐ Bring indoors any poinsettias that were set out for the summer.

GENERAL

- ☐ Watch for predictions of early frosts at higher elevations. Cover plants if necessary. Pull container plants indoors, cover plants in gardens with bed sheets, newspapers, paper bags, blankets, burlap or row covers. (Don't use plastic covers.)

- ☐ Turn the compost pile.

Poinsettias that have been saved from the previous year have lost their red, coral or white colors by now. Near the end of September, start placing the plants in a cool, dark place for 14 hours at night (approximately 5 p.m. until 7 a.m.). Expose them to light during the day. Repeat this process every day until the plant's bracts (uppermost leaves) turn color. Depending on the variety, your poinsettia will bloom after 8 to 11 weeks. The poinsettia should be colorful just in time for the holiday season.

OCTOBER
/ MAINTENANCE TIPS

PERENNIALS, ANNUALS AND BULBS

☐ Seed your wildflower garden now for spring blooming.

Seeding a wildflower garden isn't difficult.
Here are some ideas:

The garden will need at least partial sun, preferably full sun.

Prepare the soil as you would for any other garden. (*See How-To Tip on page 127.*) Make sure to get rid of any weeds or grasses.

Mix the seed with organic material like peat to provide an even distribution.

Spread the wildflower mix evenly across the prepared soil surface, going back and forth in one direction, such as north to south. Repeat, seeding and walking in the opposite direction.

Rake the seed in no deeper than ¼". Then tap down the seed so the soil is firm.

Water your wildflower garden on a regular basis so that the ground stays damp until the seeds germinate. Then water once a week, or when needed.

☐ Bring in any pots of tender perennials that you plan to overwinter.

> When planting a wildflower garden in fall, the seeds will overwinter. This means the seeds will lay dormant until spring and then start to grow. While there is some risk of the seeds being eaten by birds or animals, don't sow more than the label indicates. The mix will contain enough seed to compensate. It's also not a good idea to over-seed because the early bloomers in the mix will squeeze out the later bloomers. Be prepared, in most mixes, some of the perennial flowers won't bloom until the second year. If you don't want grasses planted with your wildflowers, check the label to make sure none are included in the mix. Ask your local garden center for the best mix for your area.

OCTOBER
MAINTENANCE TIPS

_____

_____

_____

_____

_____

_____

☐ Plant new perennials. Apply a balanced organic fertilizer. (*See How-To Tip on page 114.*)

☐ Plant hardy bulbs for spring blooming. (*See box this page*.)

☐ Buy extra spring bulbs for forcing. (*See page 65.*)

☐ If you haven't already planted pansies, plant now, along with spring flowering bulbs. In lower elevations, you can also plant ornamental kale.

☐ Dig up gladiolus, cannas and dahlias when leaves begin to turn yellow. Store them for the winter. (*See page 59.*)

☐ Mulch around perennials after the second hard frost at higher elevations. (It's too late for most rodents to nest and destroy roots.) (*See How-To Tip on page 115.*)

☐ Our fall is generally characterized by an early freeze followed by an Indian summer. To extend the season with color (and vegetables and herbs), use row covers.

TREES AND SHRUBS

☐ Continue watering trees and shrubs until the first hard freeze (even if the leaves have changed color and fallen).

Plant bulbs such as tulips, hyacinths, daffodils and crocuses in fall for blooming next spring. The soil should be well amended (*see How-To Tip on page 127*) and a little phosphorus should be added to the bottom of the hole before planting. There is a limit to the number of bulbs that can be planted per square foot: tulips – 8 to 10; crocuses – 10 to 15; and hyacinths and daffodils – 5. Try planting in groupings among the perennials and shrubs. Pay attention to when they bloom (some bloom earlier or later than others) and heights, to help you orchestrate spring color.

FALL - 57

OCTOBER
/ MAINTENANCE TIPS

☐ Plant container and balled and burlapped trees and shrubs. (*See How-To Tip on page 120.*)

☐ Tree leaves and old fruit should be raked and composted, tilled into the garden or used as mulch.

Want to make mulch out of tree leaves?
Here are some ideas:

Only till or use leaves as mulch if you are very sure they are not diseased.

Chop the leaves into small pieces so they will decompose more easily and won't blow away. You can do this by running over them with a mower.

Sprinkle slow-release nitrogen fertilizer on top of newly mulched beds. This will help soil and nutrients stay balanced.

☐ At higher elevations, wrap the trunks of all young and tender-barked trees in mid- to late-October. (*See page 63.*)

☐ Do not fertilize trees and shrubs now.

ROSES

☐ Do not prune roses. Tie down tall branches so they don't get buffeted by the wind.

In Colorado, it's necessary to "blow out" all the water in your sprinkler system each fall. This prevents the water lines from freezing and breaking during the winter. (Repairing irrigation lines is no fun!) Contact a sprinkler company to come and do the job, or rent the necessary equipment (compressor and proper attachments) at an equipment rental shop. Watch the weather. If temperatures are due to drop below freezing, flush and drain your irrigation systems, and disconnect and drain hoses and bring them inside for the winter. If you leave them connected, outside faucets can be damaged.

OCTOBER
MAINTENANCE TIPS

_____

_____

_____

_____

_____

_____

☐ Water when the soil is dry. (*See How-To Tip on page 124.*)

☐ Mulch shrub roses after the second hard frost at higher elevations. (It's too late for most rodents to nest and destroy roots.) (*See How-To Tip on page 115.*)

LAWN

☐ Check Lawn Maintenance Calendar. (*See page 150.*)

☐ Apply a winterizing fertilizer to the lawn and aerate. (*See page 114.*)

☐ Rake dead leaves off the lawn.

☐ Mow for the last time in mid-October. Mow to 2".

☐ If moisture is minimal, water your lawn.

☐ Winterize the irrigation system before a hard freeze, especially at higher elevations.

KITCHEN GARDEN

☐ Plant garlic cloves.

☐ Harvest brussel sprouts and pumpkins after the first frost. (*See page 60.*) (*See How-To Tip on page 116.*)

We need to dig up and store certain flower bulbs over the winter (gladiolus, cannas, dahlias and certain exotic daffodils). After digging, let the bulbs dry out for about one week and then store in packing material (peat moss, vermiculite, sand, sawdust) in a cool (about 50°), dry place. If the bulbs become diseased or start rotting, throw them out; if sprouting, move to a place that is colder and/or drier.

FALL - 59

OCTOBER
/ MAINTENANCE TIPS

- ☐ Harvest winter squash and gourds. (*See box this page.*)

- ☐ Pull and compost finished vegetable plants. (*See How-To Tip on page 111.*)

- ☐ At higher elevations, spade vegetable garden and add organic matter, such as finished compost.

- ☐ Put mulch around your carrots and other root crops to keep the ground from freezing. You can then continue to harvest for another couple of months.

INTERIOR PLANTS

- ☐ Thoroughly clean and prune indoor plants. (*See How-To Tip on page 111.*)

GENERAL

- ☐ If you have leaves and plant materials that you know or suspect are diseased, put them in a "hot" compost pile (140° to 160°) or discard.

Want to start a "hot" compost pile?
Here are some ideas:

You can compost diseased plant materials in a hot pile.

Discard anything you suspect has insect problems.

Harvest winter squash and gourds. Cure in a warm (75° to 85°), dry place for 10 days. Then store in a cool (50° to 55°), dry location. Many will keep until early spring. Pumpkins are ready to harvest when they are orange in color and the skin is hard. The rind should not be easily penetrated by a thumbnail. Harvesting can be done any time before a severe frost. When harvesting the pumpkin, leave several inches of stem on the stock.

OCTOBER
MAINTENANCE TIPS

Unlike a normal compost pile, you will use equal amounts of green materials (nitrogen) and brown materials (carbon) in the hot compost pile or bin. Sources of nitrogen are found in leafy plants, vegetable garden waste, grass clippings and kitchen waste. Sources of carbon are found in leaves or shredded tree and shrub branches.

Layer your materials, starting with brown and followed by green, until the pile is about 4' tall. (The first layer should be branches or something that allows for good air circulation.)

Water the pile until it is moist (not wet!).

Monitor the temperature until it reaches approximately 140°, which will take anywhere from four to seven days. When the temperature begins to decrease, turn the pile and the temperature will begin to rise again. Repeat this process once a week for two more weeks.

After turning the pile a third time, wait 1 more week and the compost should be ready to use.

☐ Water trees, shrubs and roses if needed. (*See How-To Tip on page 124.*)

☐ Turn the compost pile. (*See How-To Tip on page 111.*)

Colorado is known for its beautiful fall weather. Plants enjoy it too. Generally, winds are mild, temperatures are not extreme and the humidity is higher than usual. The result is an ideal time to plant nearly everything, with the exception of some broadleaf evergreens, warm season grasses and annuals. The roots of plants planted now will have the opportunity to establish themselves and supply the leaves with much-needed moisture in the spring. This gives the plant a healthy start for an entire growing season.

NOVEMBER
MAINTENANCE TIPS

PERENNIALS, ANNUALS AND BULBS

- ☐ If you haven't already done so, mulch around plants. (*See How-To Tip on page 115.*)

- ☐ Check stored bulbs to make sure they aren't sprouting or rotting. (*See page 59.*)

- ☐ If the ground isn't frozen, you can still plant bulbs. (They may bloom a little later than those planted in September or October but they will still bloom.)

- ☐ Cut back perennials from last year so they will bloom better.

TREES AND SHRUBS

- ☐ Mulch young or newly planted trees and shrubs. (*See How-To Tip on page 115.*) Wait until the end of the month when the ground is frozen.

- ☐ Brush heavy snow off tree and shrub limbs at higher elevations.

It's important to cut back perennials now. If the foliage is diseased, it will not only re-infect the plant next season, but it also could spread the disease to other plants. With a sharp pair of pruners, remove dead plant material all the way to the crown. Remove or compost debris.

NOVEMBER
MAINTENANCE TIPS

_____

_____

_____

_____

_____

_____

☐ Dig a hole now for planting a live Christmas tree after the holiday season. (If you wait until after the holidays, the ground may be frozen and hard to work with.) Bag the soil from the hole and add soil amendments now.

☐ Leave the snow on low-lying shrubs to act as an insulator at higher elevations.

☐ Check the guys, wiring and stakes on all trees to make sure they are not girdling, pinching or strangling the tree. Remember, tree straps should only be used temporarily, after the tree is first planted. (*See How-To Tip on page 122.*)

☐ Wrap or whitewash the trunks of young and tender-barked trees. (*See box this page.*)

☐ Protect new trees and shrubs from deer, elk and other wildlife.

Want to make sure your new trees and shrubs will survive the winter without getting eaten? Here are some ideas, if you don't want to fence:

There are liquid substances that can be rubbed on trees and shrubs that taste bad to wildlife. The liquid is safe for both the wildlife and the plant (not for edible plants though!).

Trees and shrubs exposed to the south or southwest are prone to sunscald in winter. On sunny days, temperatures in the sun can get as high as 60° and, because the tree has no leaves for protection, the tender bark will freeze and then thaw, causing cracking. To prevent sunscald, wrap the tree trunk with tree wrap or any other light-colored material that can be removed in the spring. The trunk can also be sprayed with a diluted white latex (not oil-based) paint.

FALL - 63

NOVEMBER
MAINTENANCE TIPS

Tree grates come in a variety of styles, materials and sizes.

Tree guards made of plastic tubing are usually effective. Plastic mesh tree guards can be used, but are less effective.

You can make your own protectors from chicken wire. If you use wire, be sure to remove it carefully once the tree or shrub branches start to grow through.

ROSES

☐ Mulch rose bushes in early November, or when the temperature in your yard has dropped to 22°.

LAWN

☐ Check Lawn Maintenance Calendar. (*See page 150.*)

☐ Clean and store lawn tools and lawn mower.

Here are some ideas for cleaning and storing your garden tools:

Drain the gasoline out of all equipment, or add a stabilizer.

Keep a mixture of three parts sand and one part motor oil handy to clean tools during and after the gardening season. The sand takes off dirt and debris; the oil prevents rusting.

> **To help rose bushes survive winter temperature fluctuations, mound them with mulch, such as soil, straw or wood chips. (Don't use sawdust as it blocks winter watering.) The mulch should extend from the center of the bush out, 8" high, around all canes of the bush. (This mounding should be removed in late March or April.)**

NOVEMBER
MAINTENANCE TIPS

_____

_____

_____

_____

_____

_____

Create a touch of spring during the cold winter months by "forcing" spring bulbs to grow in pots inside your home. Buy healthy tulip, hyacinth, daffodil, crocus and dwarf or Dutch iris bulbs early this month. Set the bulbs close together in shallow pots in good potting soil. The tip of the bulb should be exposed by about one-third (iris should be covered). Water thoroughly, then place the pots in a cold location (consistent 40°) for 13 to 15 weeks. Check the bulbs to see if they have developed a number of roots; if they have, the bulbs are ready to "graduate" to a warmer location (consistent 55°). As growth shoots up, move the pots to a permanent location.

Rinse out clay pots and put them where they won't freeze in winter.

After use or cleaning, put away garden tools to avoid injuries. Pegboard or hooks in the garage are a good idea.

☐ Winterize your irrigation system and drain hoses. Do it now, before the pipes freeze or your outside faucets crack. (*See page 58.*)

KITCHEN GARDEN

☐ Harvest and store potatoes now, for use over the winter.

You can store your potatoes to use over the winter. Here are some ideas:

Potatoes should only be harvested after the first fall frost. If you plan to store them, let the potatoes remain on the vine for two weeks before picking them.

You need to let potatoes "cure" by placing them in a pile in a dark area with good air circulation and a temperature of 55° to 65° for at least a week. At lower elevations, you can leave them in a pile in the garden and cover them with burlap, but protect them from rain.

To store, place potatoes in a dark, fairly humid area with a temperature of 35° to 40° (no colder than 35°).

NOVEMBER
MAINTENANCE TIPS

If potatoes turn a little sweet, leave them out in the kitchen at room temperature for about a week to restore their original flavor.

☐ Spade your vegetable garden and add organic matter which will break down by next spring. (If you mulched carrots and other root crops in October, you can continue to harvest.)

INTERIOR PLANTS

☐ Purchase bulbs for forcing and indoor winter blooming. (*See page 65.*)

☐ For continuous blooming of forced bulbs throughout the winter, only "graduate" one or two pots per week from a 40° location to a 50° location. The bulbs can remain in the 40° location for several months.

☐ In mid-November, pot bulbs for holiday blooming. (*See box this page.*)

☐ Bring out amaryllis to begin forcing bloom.

GENERAL

☐ Create and build a rock garden. (*See list on page 146.*)

☐ Turn the compost pile. (*See How-To Tip on page 111.*)

> Some bulbs, like paperwhites and amaryllis, do not have to be placed in the cold for 13 to 15 weeks before they will bloom. Simply pot the bulbs and care for as you would any houseplant. Paperwhites will bloom about five weeks after planting; amaryllis in about eight weeks.

WINTER

DECEMBER
MAINTENANCE TIPS

_____

_____

_____

_____

_____

_____

_____

PERENNIALS, ANNUALS AND BULBS

☐ Check stored bulbs to make sure they aren't sprouting or rotting. (*See page 59.*)

☐ Spread evergreen branches throughout the garden beds and in pots to give a festive feel to the landscape and to provide extra protection for plants.

TREES AND SHRUBS

☐ A miniature tree (bonsai) in a nice pot makes a unique and appreciated gift any time of year. Check with your local garden center to be sure the chosen tree can be kept indoors year round.

☐ Add lighting to your landscape.

☐ Plant your live Christmas tree in the hole dug in November.

☐ Live Christmas trees should not be left inside for more than five days or the tree may start to put on new growth. The shock will be too great after the tree is moved outside and it could die.

There are several basic rules when adding lighting to your home landscape. Do not put in "runway" lighting (a term for lining your driveway or sidewalk with lights) because all you create is a focus on the lights themselves, not aspects of the landscape. Remember, the areas that are left dark are as important as those you light – contrast is visually appealing. Start with lighting in or around trees. You can hide the lighting source and at the same time move the lighting away from the house for more visual appeal. Put lights on the ground shining up, under trees or create "moon" lighting by hiding the light fixtures up in your trees.

WINTER - 69

DECEMBER
MAINTENANCE TIPS

ROSES

☐ If you haven't mounded your rose bushes with 8"plus of mulch, it still isn't too late. (*See How-To Tip on page 115.*)

INTERIOR PLANTS

☐ Place your poinsettia where it will receive as much indoor light as possible. Keep it moist and don't allow it to dry out.

How should you care for a poinsettia?
Here are some ideas:

Poinsettias are one of the most common holiday plant purchases. If cared for, a poinsettia will bloom for several months and keep its leaves until summer.

Put poinsettias in a place where the nighttime temperature won't drop below a consistent 60°. Daytime temperature should be consistent and not exceed 80°.

☐ The decorative foil plant sleeves that come with plants such as poinsettias, azaleas and Christmas cactus prevent the pot from draining easily after watering. Poke a few holes in the sleeve, or get rid of it altogether, and put the plant in a nice basket or a larger pot.

> Before bringing a potted live Christmas tree into the house, first keep it in a somewhat cold place (preferably a garage) for two days. Once inside, place the tree in a cool, dry spot away from direct sunlight and heating ducts. Put it in a container large enough to fit the root ball and cover with some type of mulch, such as wood chips. Keep the root ball moist. Move the tree to the garage for several days to harden off. Then plant your live Christmas tree (*see How-To Tip on page 120*) in the hole prepared in November. Thoroughly water the tree after planting and again each month until spring (*see How-To Tip on page 124*).

DECEMBER
MAINTENANCE TIPS

_____

_____

_____

_____

_____

_____

_____

Keep a cut Christmas tree outside in a bucket of water until you are ready to bring it inside. Cut several inches off the bottom of the trunk and water it. The best thing you can do to help a cut tree last is to give it plenty of water, especially during the first week. Another remedy to help your tree last longer is to mix a solution of 1/2 cup of bleach, 2 tablespoons of sugar and 1 gallon of water. Pour the mixture into the tree basin and refill as necessary. The bleach kills bacteria in the basin and the sugar and water helps to prevent the needles from drying out.

☐ A Christmas cactus is a great plant for the holidays.

How should you care for a Christmas cactus? Here are some ideas:

To help your Christmas cactus bloom, the plant should be kept in a sunny location, but not in direct sunlight.

It also will bloom better when kept in a place where the temperatures are about 50° to 55° at night.

Keep the plant away from any kind of hot air.

A Christmas cactus doesn't need a lot of water. Don't overwater your Christmas cactus during November and December.

If you fertilize, use a low nitrogen, high phosphorus mixture (10-30-10).

☐ Bring potted spring bulbs into a warmer (55°), light location for forcing at the end of this month. (*See page 65.*)

☐ Reduce watering houseplants as the days become shorter. They can be overwatered if you are watering as much as you do in late spring, summer and early fall.

WINTER - 71

DECEMBER
MAINTENANCE TIPS

☐ If you haven't started forcing an amaryllis, you can do it early this month.

GENERAL

☐ Fresh cut Christmas trees should not be left in the house for more than three weeks. (*See page 71.*)

☐ Garden tools make great gifts for gardeners. Plus, many garden centers offer discounts on tools at this time of year

Give your friends a garden basket for the holidays. Here are some ideas:

A trowel and/or leather gardening gloves are always welcome additions to a gardening basket.

Instead of using a basket as a container for everything, why not a big, floppy straw hat?

☐ Set out food for birds that may call your garden home. (*See box this page.*)

☐ If moisture is below normal, make certain to water trees, shrubs and your lawn. (*See How-To Tip on page 124.*)

☐ If moisture is below normal, continue to water the compost pile.

Location, location, location. A bird feeder should be placed where you can see the birds, but not near trees because the food will encourage squirrels. If possible, put the feeder near a protected overhang, but not so close to the windows that birds will fly into them. Suet and black oil sunflower seed are popular among most species of birds. Providing water to your feathered friends is a nice bonus, but you will have to contend with ice and freezing each day. If you plan to feed the birds, be committed – for their sake!

DECEMBER
MAINTENANCE TIPS

_____

_____

_____

_____

_____

_____

Winter watering is important. Here are some ideas:

Check the ground several inches down and, if it's dry, then water. (Overwatering isn't good for the plants either!)

Don't let water puddle, especially if it could freeze and turn to ice.

Water midday (between 10 a.m. and 2 p.m.) when temperatures are near 50° and the ground is not frozen (or at higher elevations, not covered with snow).

Here are some thoughts and ideas about winter composting:

In Colorado, it's usually not warm enough for the decomposition process to take place in winter, so composting stops during winter months.

Composting will resume in early March, so begin watering again at that time.

Don't add materials to the pile during winter. Any materials added will freeze and smell when decomposition begins again.

To compost during winter months, consider trying a redworm composting bin inside, using kitchen waste.

Decorate with plants and blossoms from the garden during December. Grapevines, Virginia creeper and silverlace all make beautiful runners and window trimmings. Cornstalks, ornamental corn, dried gourds or some of the flowers from your garden that you dried in the fall will provide welcome touches. Holly berries, rose hips and the berries from cranberry cotoneasters are a beautiful complement to other decorations. Arrangements can be made using twigs from shrubs such as Apache plume (white branches), red twig dogwood (red branches) and Oregon grape.

WINTER - 73

JANUARY
MAINTENANCE TIPS

PERENNIALS, ANNUALS AND BULBS

☐ Check stored bulbs for signs of dryness or rotting. (*See page 59.*)

☐ Check to make sure the mulch is still covering plants that are exposed to the south and southwest.

☐ If you didn't get around to this in December, protect plants by laying evergreen branches from Christmas trees on perennial beds, areas where bulbs are planted and around rose bushes.

Plan and buy materials for a topiary that you can start inside from seed in February. Here is one idea:

Plant a combination of morning glories, hops, moonflowers, four o'clocks and nasturtiums in a large pot. (You can do this in a smaller pot, too – just plant fewer.) Follow the spacing instructions.

Once the plants are growing, invert a tomato cage (or any other open wire or plastic structure that the plants can be "trained" to climb) and attach it to the top of your pot.

As the plants grow, "train" them (gently guide them) to grow up the structure on top of the pot.

> The following companies are good choices for ordering short-season vegetable seeds: D.V. Burrell's, 719-254-3318; Johnny's Select Seeds, 207-437-9294, www.johnnyseeds.com; High Altitude Gardens, 208-788-4363, www.seedsave.org; Vesey's Seeds Ltd., 800-363-7333, www.veseys.com; The Cook's Garden, 800-457-9703, www.cooksgarden.com; Burpee Seeds & Plants, 800-888-1447, www.burpee.com; Shepherd's Garden Seeds, 800-503-9624, www.shepherdseeds.com; Plants of the Southwest, 800-788-7333, www.plantsofthesouthwest.com; and Lake Valley, 707-642-4167 www.midcitynursery.com.

JANUARY
MAINTENANCE TIPS /

_____

_____

_____

_____

_____

_____

_____

> Rotating the location of where you plant your vegetables each year in your kitchen garden is important for two reasons. First, any disease that doesn't die out over the winter won't easily spread to a different family of vegetables in the next growing season. Second, different families of vegetables use different nutrients from the soil. Rotating will prevent reduction of those nutrients from the same places in the garden. Rotate cabbage family (cabbage, brussel sprouts and turnips), solanaceae family (tomatoes, potatoes and peppers), alliums (garlic and onions), corn, beans and peas.

When the weather is warmer, move your topiary outside.

☐ Plan for a Winter Garden next season.

Colorado has four distinctly different seasons and each can bring gardening enjoyment. Here are some Winter Garden ideas:

Only plan for what you can see, either from inside or as a focal point in front of your home.

A Winter Garden needs a lot of structure. Incorporate not only plants, but rocks, stone, water features and garden art.

Evergreen shrubs form a nice basis for the garden. Arrange several specialty conifers together. They come in different sizes, shapes, textures and hues of green and blue.

After establishing structure, fill in the landscape with shrub roses, ornamental grasses or plants with colorful branches. (*See the list on page 146.*)

A Winter Garden is especially spectacular when it is lighted. (*See page 69.*)

TREES AND SHRUBS

☐ Gently brush the snow off trees and shrubs if you live at higher elevations.

WINTER - 75

JANUARY
MAINTENANCE TIPS

☐ Apply dormant oil spray when temperature is above 32°.

ROSES

☐ Review catalogs for purchasing roses from mail order sources or your local garden center.

KITCHEN GARDEN

☐ Review seed catalogs for short season or new and exciting vegetable varieties. (*See page 74.*)

☐ Plan a container herb garden or windowbox.

There are some considerations for planning a container herb garden. Here are some ideas:

Order the seeds now; sow the seeds indoors in February.

Move the containers outdoors when the weather permits. (Herb gardens can be grown indoors, but they are easier to tend and less trouble outdoors.)

Container herb gardens can be grown in almost any space where you can put the container. They are suitable for people who have trouble getting around a larger garden. They can be planted on balconies, rooftops and in windowboxes.

___

To really clean the leaves of houseplants, combine 1 ounce of vegetable oil and 23 ounces of water and mix well. Spray the leaves of the plants. It's not necessary to wipe them afterward, but if you do, support each leaf underneath with your hand and wipe carefully with terrycloth. You can also wear an old sock like a mitt and wipe down the plants. Caution: Some houseplants, such as those with hairy leaves, may not like this treatment (try one or two leaves first).

JANUARY
MAINTENANCE TIPS /

_____

_____

_____

_____

_____

_____

It's important that you fertilize interior plants with only a slow-release fertilizer because it will not really take effect until the plants need it – beginning in late March or April. Slightly reduce the amount of water you are giving houseplants now because daylight hours are minimal and plants need less water now. Overwatering can lead to problems like fungus gnat infestations.

If you're going to eventually harvest the herbs, it's practical to plant one variety per container. If you want mostly "show," then plant a variety of herbs in one large container.

Don't overfill the pot. Follow the package's spacing instructions.

As with any garden, don't plant shade-loving herbs together with sun-loving herbs – if you do, one of them will suffer.

Your container should have holes in the sides (preferable) or bottom, for proper drainage.

If you use good potting soil, found at your local garden center, you don't need to put rocks in the bottom of the container.

☐ Plan to rotate your kitchen garden vegetables every two years. (*See page 75.*)

☐ Plan an outdoor herb garden.

Here are some considerations when planting an outdoor herb garden:

As with all edible gardens, be sure the herb garden is easy to get to and there is a water source nearby.

Herbs need at least a half day of sun (more is preferable).

JANUARY
MAINTENANCE TIPS

Amend the soil as with flower beds, but keep in mind that it is particularly important with herbs that the soil drains well. Most herbs thrive in dryer environments.

Taller plants should be planted to the inside (if you can get to the garden from all sides) or to the back. Shorter plants should be planted to the outside or in the front.

Don't plant perennial herbs too close together or they will become overcrowded the next growing season.

INTERIOR PLANTS

☐ Clean the leaves of houseplants. (*See box page 76.*)

☐ Fertilize all houseplants with a slow-release fertilizer. (*See box page 77.*)

GENERAL

☐ Use kitty-litter, sand or birdseed on driveways and icy paths. Do not use salt or chemicals that can build up in the soil and eventually cause problems for plants.

☐ Leave the compost pile alone.

☐ If moisture is less than normal, you will need to water your trees, shrubs, lawn and possibly roses. (*See How-To Tip on page 124.*)

If you own a water feature, the frequency and amount that you seed it with a dry bacteria is determined by the type of system and the time of year. Seed at least twice a year. Purchase the dry bacteria from a hardware store or garden center. With a clean coffee can or small bucket, scoop some water out of the feature and add the bacteria to the water per directions on the product. Stir and let stand for a few minutes. Then pour the mixture into your water feature. Bacteria is a vital part of your water feature because it helps to keep the water clean and establish the ecosystem.

DESIGNS

WATER GARDEN

WATER GARDEN

KEY

1. Ponderosa pine
2. Blue mist spirea
2a. Bristlecone pine
3. Crimson pygmy barberry
4. Daphne
5. Froebel spirea
6. Gold mound spirea
6a. Globe dwarf spruce
7. Spreading juniper
8. Mugo pine
9. Ornamental grass
10. Perennials
11. Red twig dogwood
12. Shadblow
12a. Scotch broom
13. Burkwood viburnum
14. Western river birch
15. Yellow twig dogwood
16. Perennials and groundcovers
17. Autumn blaze maple
18. Boulders – Native boulders
19. Bench – Flagstone bench
20. Path – Random flagstone path
21. Bridge

NOTE / The Water Feature Garden is located on a sloped or bermed corner.

WATER GARDEN

Can't you just picture it? You've created your own private Eden with a pond, a waterfall or a small fountain surrounded by beautiful plants and trees.

BENEFITS / Water features create a peaceful setting. The calming sound of water helps you focus your attention on what is pleasant and peaceful, rather than on traffic, airplanes or other less pleasant noises in your environment.

STRUCTURE / Make the water garden the focal point of your yard. Add a stream between pools, lighting, a sitting area or a bridge to increase interest. Location is very important. A natural gentle slope is perfect, but soil also can be built up into berms to accommodate upper pools and waterfalls. Place the water garden in a location where it can be seen from inside the house, so it can be enjoyed in all seasons.

There are generally two types of water features. Some are more formal, with a lot of concrete and quarried rocks. More often, in Colorado, you will see informal water features that appear to be a natural part of the environment. Pea gravel and river cobble can be used to create a more natural look inside and along the borders of the pond. Grade first, then place boulders around the water feature so that natural runoff will not flow into the pond. Mud, lawn fertilizers and insecticides can contaminate the water and kill fish and plants.

The site should receive at least five or six hours of sunlight for best success with water plants and surrounding plantings. Keep year-round interest, succession of color and variation of texture and shape in mind when choosing plants. Character pines and dwarf spruce make lovely additions to water gardens. Avoid plantings of large and messy shrubs or trees adjacent to the edge of the pond, because they drop excessive debris in the water.

Common gold fish and Koi are the types of fish used for water gardens. Don't add fish until the pool water has "cured" for a month. Fish should not be fed when the water temperature is below 50°. A small stock tank heater can be used in winter to keep a section of the pond's surface unfrozen so fish will not suffocate.

The lowest pond should always be the largest, and capable of holding the contents of the upper ponds and stream without overflowing when the waterfall is not in operation. A good size for the lower pond is about 10' by 15'. The minimum depth of a pond should be around 2.5' to 3' to successfully overwinter fish. Shelves or planting pockets can be created at the sides of the pond to hold water plants needing 18" in depth.

WATER GARDEN

SOIL AND SOIL AMENDMENTS / Amend the soil around your water feature as you would for any of your gardens (*see page 127*) with one exception. It's important to remove any sharp rocks or roots that can puncture the liner during installation.

INSECTS AND DISEASES / Be aware and plan for the fact that critters like water, especially if you have fish. Heron and raccoons especially prey on garden fish. Also, remember that some plants can become very invasive in water settings because the water is conductive to their growth.

CONSTRUCTION TIPS / Two choices when deciding on the type of pool construction are a liner with a tinted concrete overlay or just the liner. Tinted concrete pools are more durable and look very natural when landscaped. If concrete is not used, the liner should be Butyl or EPDM rubber. Both are very flexible and easy to install. Use padding beneath the liner to protect it from puncture by rocks and roots.

It is important that the pump size accommodate the pond and the vertical elevation that water must be pumped. For best results, place a skimmer on the opposite side of the waterfall in the lowest pool to capture any debris before it settles and clogs the pump or sours the water.

There are several filtration systems: gravity-fed biological filters, mechanical biological filters and sand filters (more expensive but easy to maintain because they don't have mats). If you install filters that require mats, they must be cleaned at least twice a year.

Water features should be allowed to run even in winter. Ice forming on waterfalls and fountains is particularly interesting. Make sure the waterline below the ice is sufficient for pump operation.

XERISCAPE GARDEN

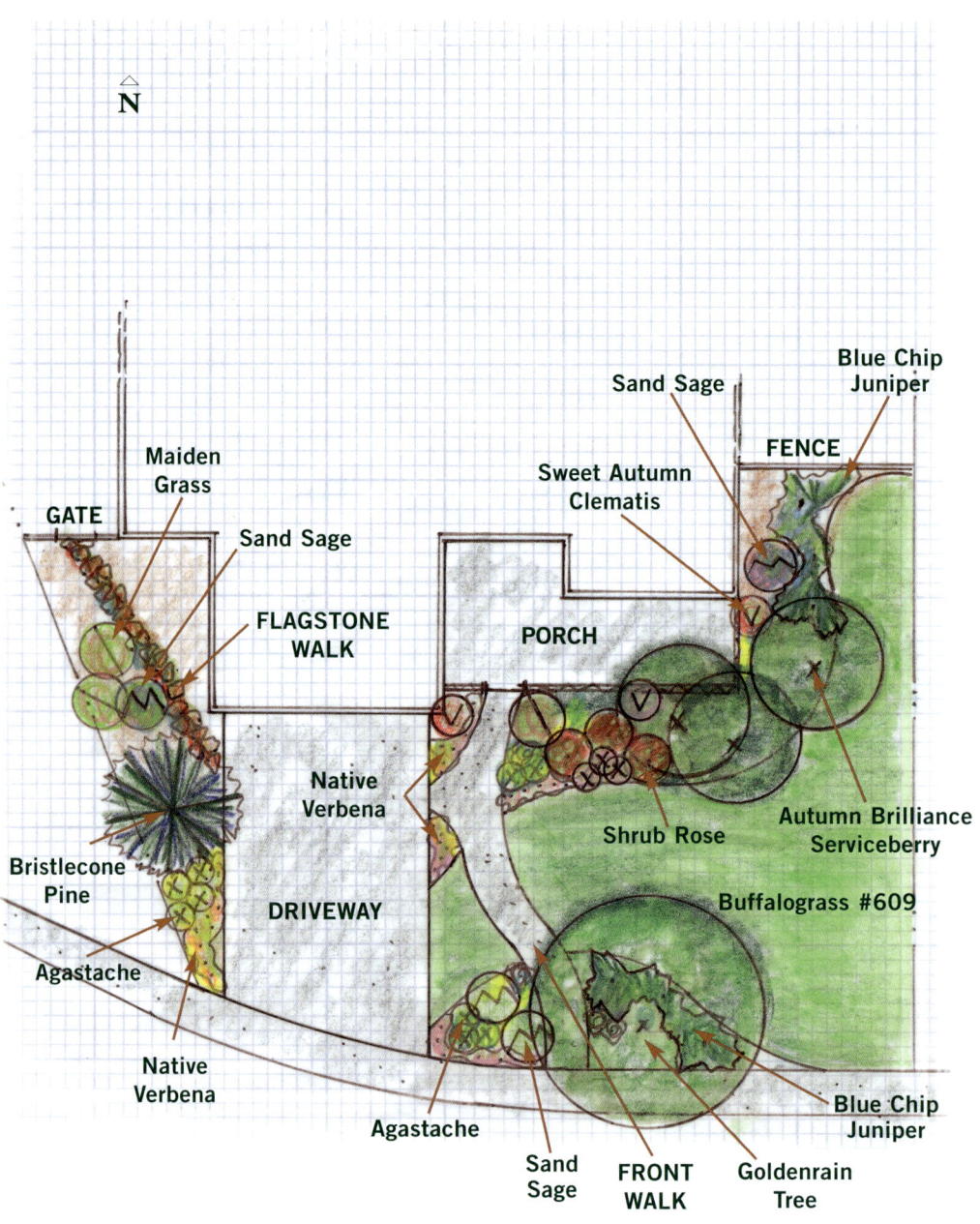

XERISCAPE GARDEN

Xeriscaping refers to water-efficient landscaping. The root word "xeric" is Greek for "dry." Because our state receives relatively little moisture, the "xeric" approach to landscaping has become quite popular in recent years.

BENEFITS / Less is more. A Xeriscape garden takes less maintenance, requires less money and is an ecologically sound way to garden in Colorado, requiring less water and fewer fertilizers and chemicals. A Xeriscape garden also provides a great habitat for birds and wildlife.

STRUCTURE / Take a look at what Mother Nature has done and you will find the basic structural components that can form your xeriscape garden. Use small amounts of sod or turf; design to flow with the natural landscape; and place plants based upon where they grow naturally (north, south, east, west). Place shrubs in groupings, plant flowers together in designated beds and use plants that don't need much water. Taller shade trees conserve energy; smaller evergreen trees can be effective screens and look good year-round.

SOIL AND SOIL AMENDMENTS / For buffalograss, work the soil down about 6", no amending is needed. If you have to use Kentucky bluegrass or tall fescue, work the soil down about 6", amending with compost or sphagnum peat. In flower beds, rototill and work the soil down about 10" to 12". Amend the soil with a compost and peat moss mix. Shrubs can be planted to the size of the ball or container, no amending is needed.

INSECTS AND DISEASES / For powdery mildew, cut back the foliage on the plants when they are done blooming and remove all fallen leaves.

A Special Note / Don't cover your landscape with Kentucky bluegrass! Instead, think about using buffalograss, at least in the backyard areas. Buffalograss uses about 60% less water than Kentucky bluegrass (which requires 24" of water per year), it looks good with minimal watering and requires about 75% less mowing than bluegrass.

KITCHEN GARDEN

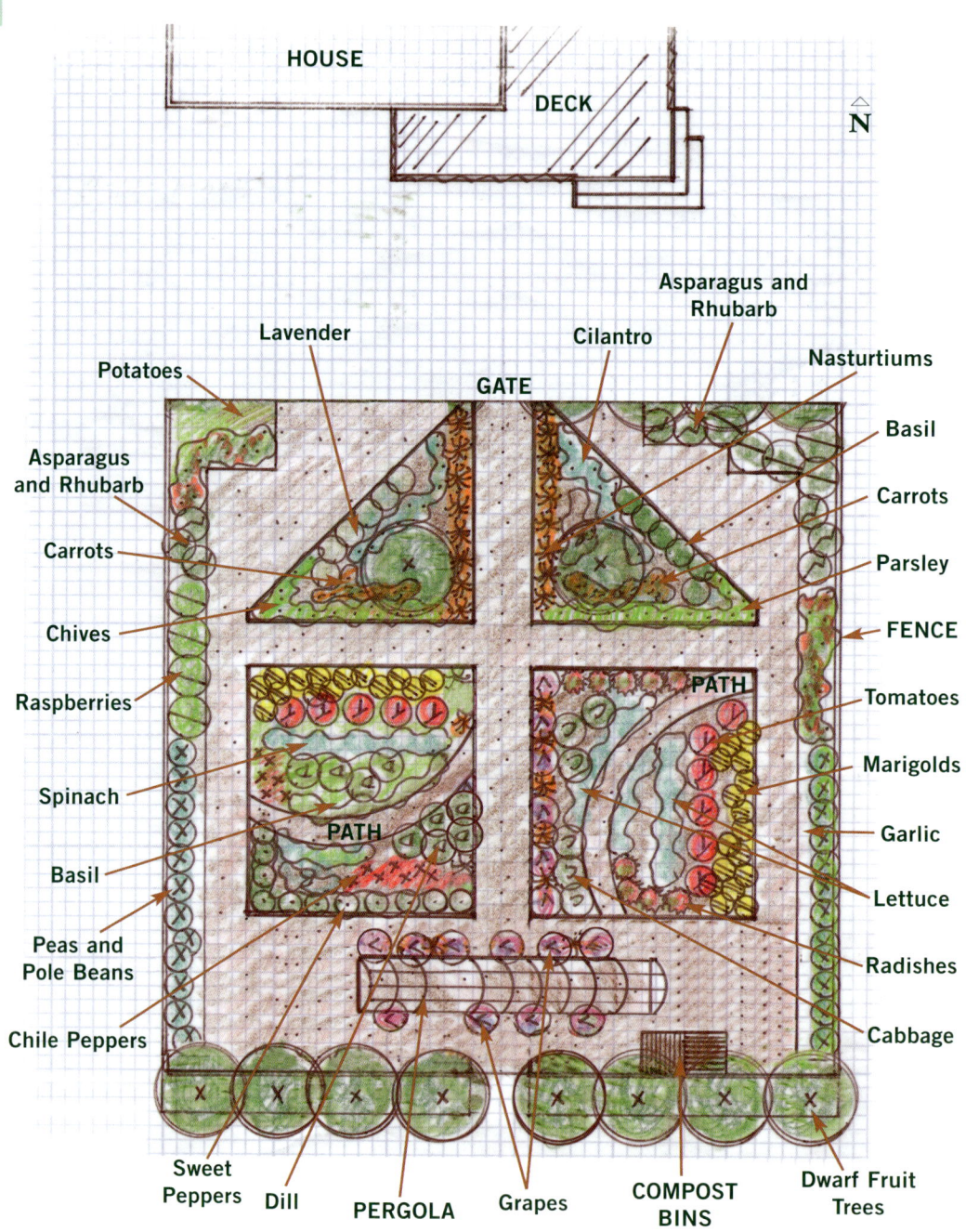

KITCHEN GARDEN

A kitchen garden is a feel-good garden. It's rewarding to put little transplants in the ground, care for them, watch them grow and finally produce something you can actually eat (or give to your friends to eat). And, believe it or not, a garden of vegetables and herbs is one of the easiest to grow.

STRUCTURE / Find a level area in your yard, preferably near the house so it's easier to tend and close to a water source. (Plus, you can watch your garden grow.) You want the garden to get full sun for at least eight hours each day during the spring and summer months. Adding pathways provides space for walking, weeding and harvesting.

Seed catalogs are a good way to find vegetables and herbs that you might like to grow. Then go to your garden center and buy transplants, unless you have the time to start your plants from seed indoors. If the garden center doesn't carry what you want, ask questions. It may be that your choice for a plant doesn't grow well here.

Basic (or "hot" season) vegetables like warmer summer temperatures and are ready after the first frost. "Cool" season vegetables grow best in the cooler temperatures common in early spring and late fall. After two or three seasons of gardening, you will understand the vegetables and herbs you like to grow well enough to plant succession crops.

A good mulch would be 2" to 3" of seed-free straw on the top of newspaper. You can sprinkle grass clippings over this during the growing season to add nitrogen to the soil and help control weeds. Don't use grass clippings from a chemically treated lawn. You also can mulch with wood chips, but use these sparingly because they change soil chemistry over time.

WATERING / Water your garden daily during the hottest days of the summer and every other day during the cooler months. Plants like direct watering, especially in the hottest, driest months of summer. You also can give plants different amounts of water. For example, corn and cucumbers like lots of water, while herbs do better with less. The best time to water is early in the morning, before 10 a.m. This also helps conserve water.

A Special Note / Plant flowers in and among your vegetables and herbs, lining the perimeter and pathways of your kitchen garden. Some plants, like nasturtiums and dill, are not only edible, but serve as great insect disrupters. In addition, the flowers can be spiritually and aesthetically pleasing to the senses.

WHIMSICAL GARDEN

WHIMSICAL GARDEN

The whimsical garden reflects a spirit of fun and creativity. Each whimsical garden is unique, reflecting the spirit of its maker. Underlying every whimsical garden is practical garden design, construction and maintenance.

Start your whimsical garden with a strong site plan. Consider scale (Is this a patio home or a ranch?), grading (Does water pool anywhere? Do you need to retain slopes?), orientation (What is the sun/shade exposure of the high-use areas?) and use (Do you play touch football regularly or raise prize-winning roses?). Carefully think through your site plan. Getting the basic, big ticket items in the right place and at the right size the first time around saves money and makes you happy, setting the stage for whimsy.

Set the whimsical garden character by selecting high-quality construction materials and building things right. If the building skills available to you are limited, choose a simple design. A well-executed, simple design will enhance the whimsy in your garden. Artful details don't cover up poor-quality construction. Always do the best you can on basics.

"Grow" your whimsy by planting for your site. Don't try to grow English ivy in full sun or sun flowers in the shade (sick plants aren't whimsical). Maximize your growing success with irrigation – options include drip, micro-spray and laser drip technology. Update your clock for state-of-the-art irrigation programming. Use interesting foliage (variegated euonymus) or an interesting form (globe spruces) to enliven a potentially bland foundation planting. Pop in a crazy plant, like a spiraled juniper, a Red Hot Poker or a globe thistle for genuine Dr. Seuss whimsy. Don't forget to smell the roses, the lilacs and the Carlesii viburnum.

Details, details, details. Art and ornament don't make a whimsical garden, but you can't make a whimsical garden without them. Garden centers are awash in nifty decorative items. Buy some. Little things aren't always the most whimsical. Use sculpture boldly. Art doesn't lose its leaves in the winter.

Light it up. Night lighting can accent a special artwork or lead you along a favorite path. Varying the lighting locations (from above or below), brightness and fixtures creates nighttime magic while keeping your house and garden safer.

Finally, trust yourself. This is your garden. Go for it. If your garden isn't fun, why bother?

ROSE GARDEN /

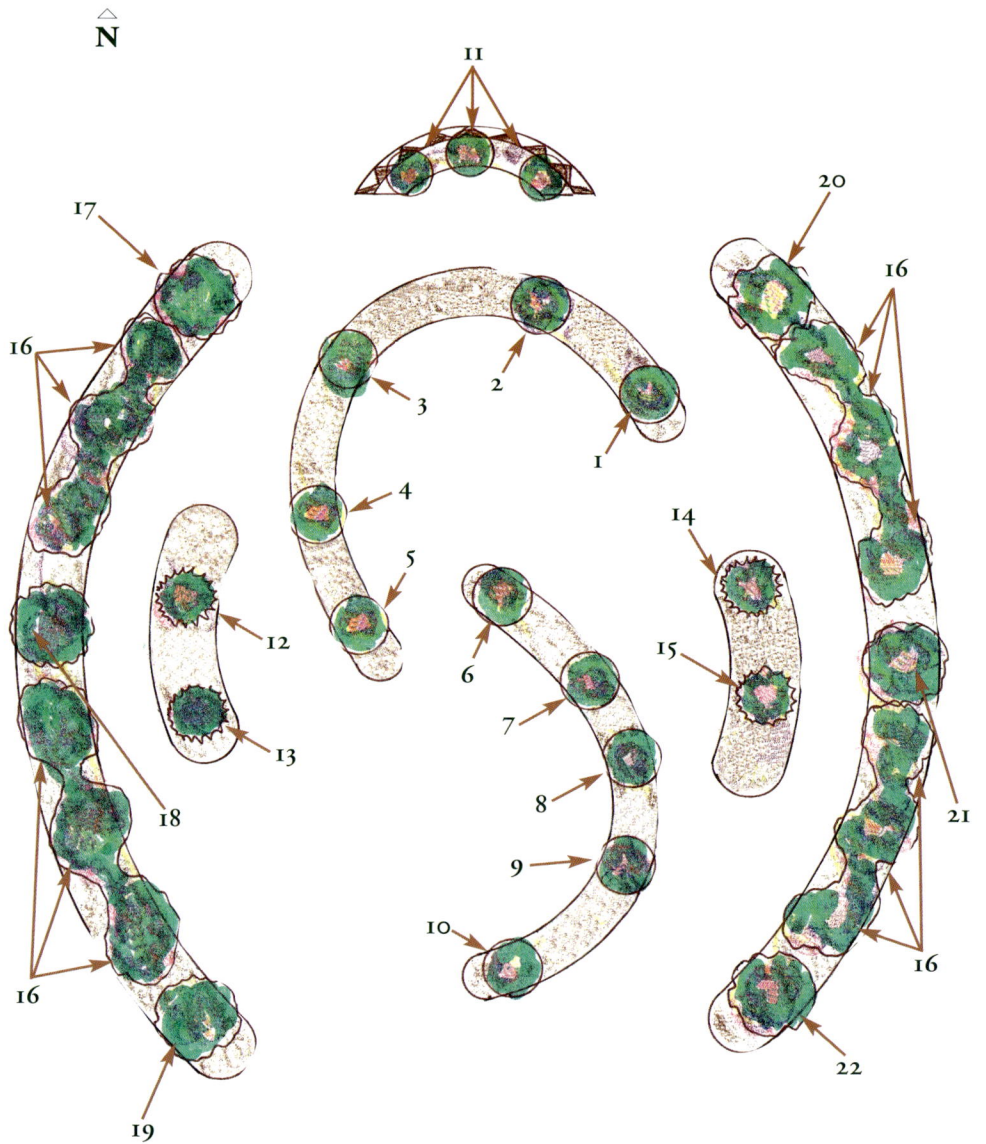

ROSE GARDEN

Roses have a reputation for being one of the harder shrubs to grow – it's not true. Roses need some care, but they will grow here, and beautifully. There's more to roses than the hybrid teas – consider the rugosas, the old garden shrub and species roses, the damasks and the albas. (*Note: the old-fashioned varieties have fewer insects and disease problems.*) Roses can be a year-round contributor to the landscape.

BENEFITS / Rose bushes come in all shapes, textures, colors and sizes. They are a versatile plant, content to form the background, eager to create a focal point or agreeable to simply exist and provide a little diversion in the landscape.

Roses can be used other than for show or as cut flowers. The hips, particularly, on some shrubs are magnificent. They create their own showcase in the landscape, or can be cut for use on wreaths or other arrangements. Rose petals, when dried, smell wonderful – add them to potpourri.

STRUCTURE / Roses do best when they are planted in locations where they get over six hours of full sun every day. They also do better planted in their own beds, alone, primarily because maintenance is similar and therefore easier. There are exceptions. Some roses, like a semi-sprawler or climber, do nicely around trees because they like both shade and sun. Some roses are not as hardy as others. This doesn't mean you can't plant them, it just means a little more work. Climbing roses are an example.

When considering which roses to plant, think about year-round color and texture. Some, like the species roses, have beautiful fall foliage. The rugosas, which also provide fall color, have tremendous hips that will last into the winter months.

A Special Note / Before buying rose bushes, see them first! Go to a local garden center or nursery, or visit places where roses are featured to see what appeals to your senses.

KEY

Hybrid Tea, Grandiflora and Floribunda Roses (plant 3' apart)
1. Mister Lincoln (dark red)
2. Peace (yellow/shaded pink)
3. Chicago Peace (coral/shaded yellow)
4. Pascali (white)
5. Chrysler Imperial (dark red)
6. Pristine (white pink edged)
7. Queen Elizabeth (medium pink)
8. Double Delight (red/white)
9. Sutter's Gold (orange blend)
10. Garden Party

Climbing Rose (plant 2' to 3' apart)
11. America (orange pink)

KEY

Miniature Roses (plant 1½' to 2' apart)
12. Easter Morning (white)
13. Rise-n-Shine (medium yellow)
14. Stars-n-Stripes (red/white striped)
15. Starina (orange red)

Groundcover Rose (plant 3' apart)
16. White Flower Carpet

Shrub Roses (plant 5' apart)
17. Rockin Robin (red and white)
18. Linda Campbell (medium red)
19. Golden Wings (light yellow)
20. 'Coral' Meidiland
21. Sharifa Asma (light pink)
22. Rosa Rugosa Alba (white)

CONTAINER GARDEN

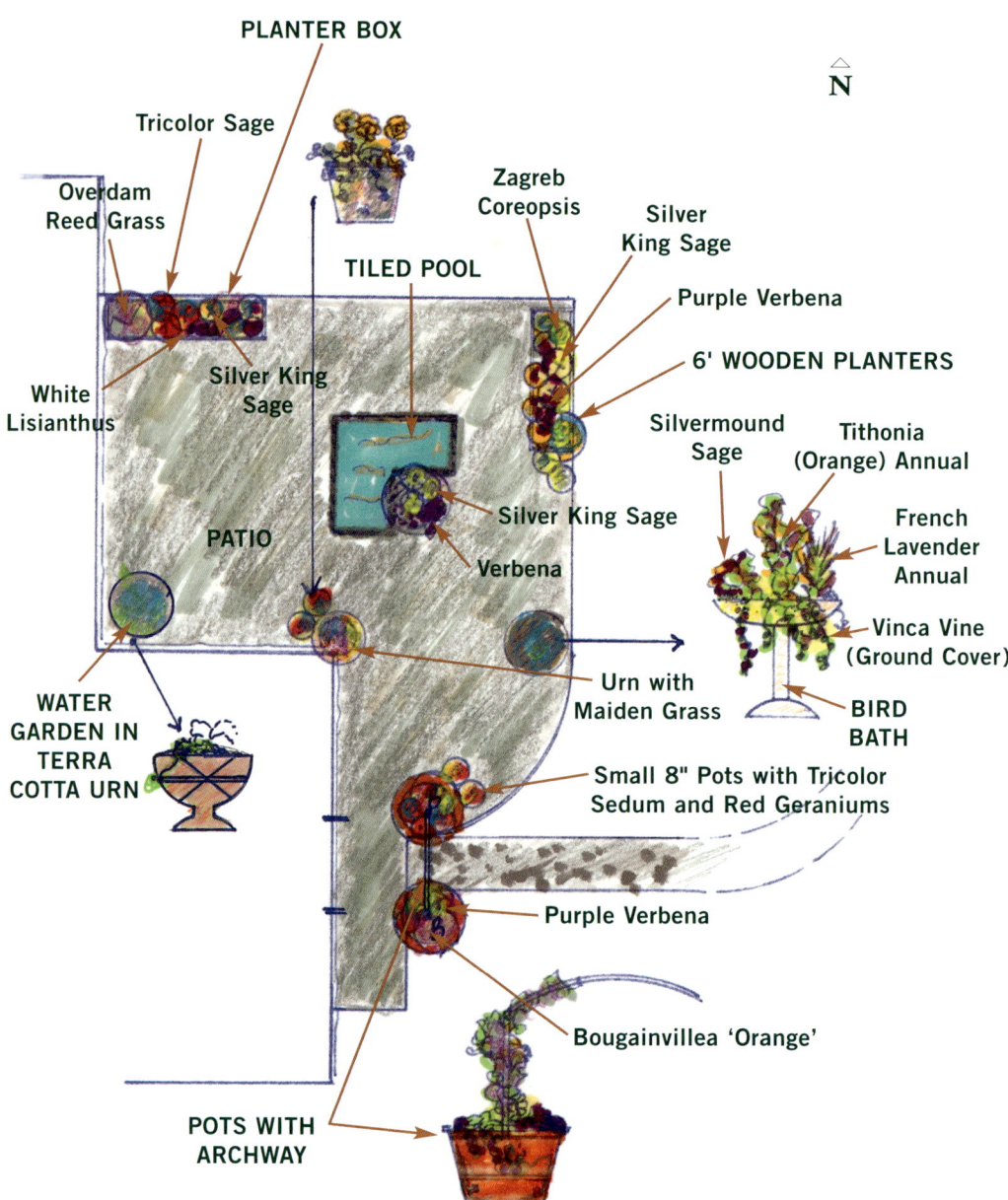

CONTAINER GARDEN

Your container garden should be an experience – to create, to plant, to nurture and to enjoy. You can try things that you would never attempt in your garden beds. Be adventuresome! Or whimsical! Or fanciful! If something isn't working, just do a little rearranging and you have a new look.

The container garden shown here has several unique elements. You might try just one of them as a focal point and then plant surrounding containers based on your available time and energy level.

The 14" terra cotta urn to the far left contains a water garden. Line it with 32ml. PVC and glue it to the urn. Set a small bubbler fountain and pump inside, and add a water plant, like a water lily.

The pathway leading to the garden at the bottom of the design features two Italian terra cotta pots that support a copper archway between them. Planted in each pot are bougainvillea vines that will grow up the copper tubing, forming an arbor.

The bird bath to the right of the design is made of stained concrete and planted with herbs and vines.

The in-ground pool in the upper middle area of the patio is shallow, only 8" deep. It is lined with vivid blue glazed tiles that are frost resistant.

Above the pool, to the left, is a 6' redwood planter box. It features a rock garden, complete with interesting rocks from a nearby quarry, and is planted with portulaca moss roses, ornamental grass and herbs.

WILDLIFE GARDEN

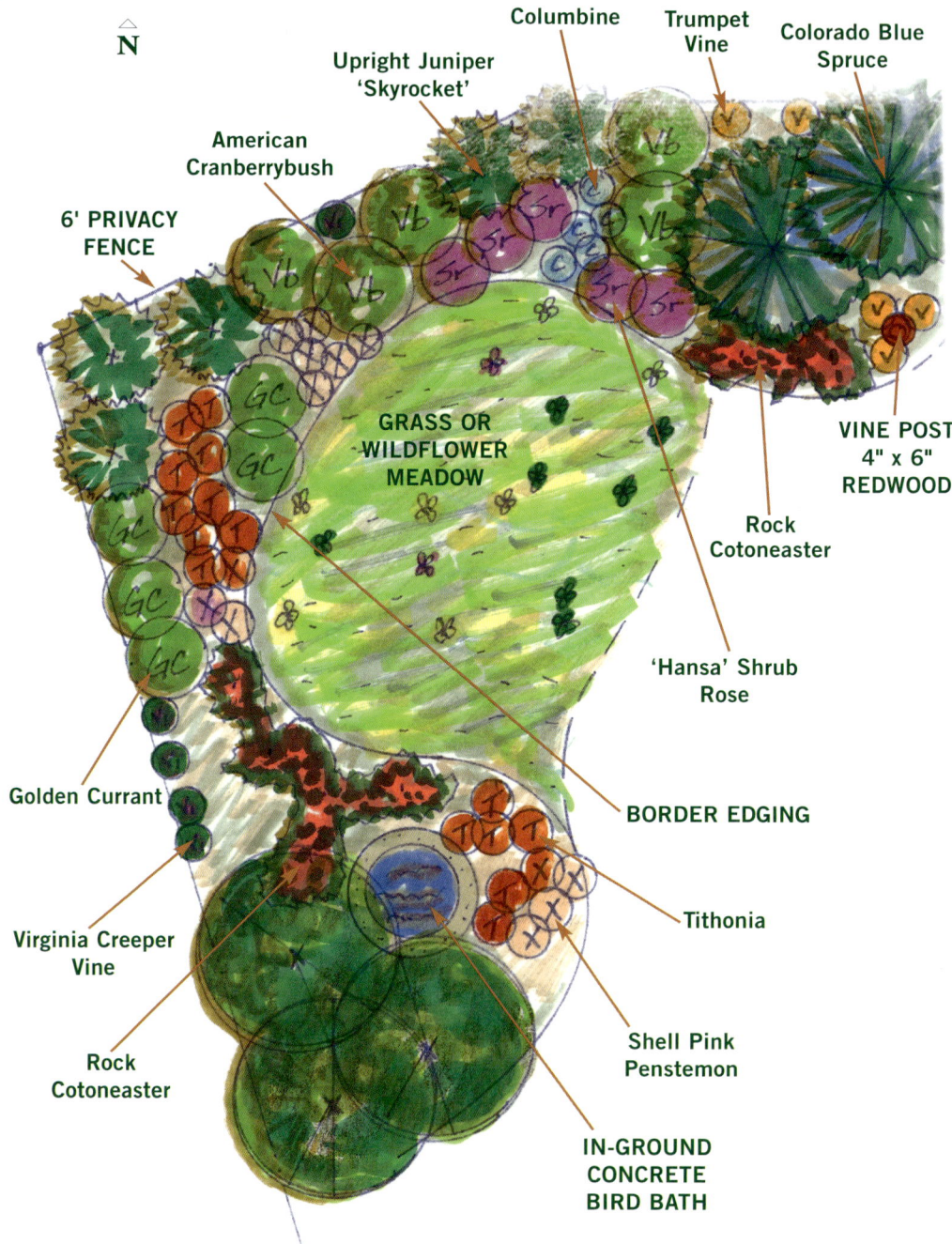

WILDLIFE GARDEN

A wildlife garden is a backyard habitat. Designed and planted correctly, you can sit outside in your own private wildlife sanctuary and feel that you are miles from home, with only the birds, the bees and the butterflies for company.

STRUCTURE / Wildlife gardens can be created from any existing location, such as a suburban backyard. The goal is to create an environment that will provide food, water and shelter for birds, butterflies and bees.

The best design is what nature provides. If you copy Mother Nature, it's more ecologically sound and will attract the wildlife. Create shelter with shrubs that have sweeping branches. Shrubs, trees and perennials provide different heights. Layers are necessary to meet the varied needs of the wildlife. (A wren has different requirements than a robin, for instance.) Screening provided by taller trees in the background provides a wind buffer for butterflies.

Plants that offer plenty of branches and nesting materials are important. Food sources can be berries, seeds, nectar and pollen from flowers, shrubs, grasses and trees. Butterflies and bees need particular types of flowers to land on for their food. Butterflies prefer fragrant plants with tight clusters of flowers. Bees are important for plant pollination (be careful when using pesticides as many are toxic to bees).

INSECTS AND DISEASES / It's important when designing and creating a wildlife garden to look toward the native plants in your area. If you use native plant materials, you will have fewer problems with diseases, and pests will be controlled through natural predators attracted by the wildlife.

A Special Note / More adventurous gardeners might consider including bats and reptiles in their plans. Consider adding a bat house to your garden. A bat can eat 500 insects a night. Turtles, lizards, snakes, frogs and salamanders also prey on insects and rodents. They will be attracted to pools and ponds.

WINDOWBOX HERB GARDEN

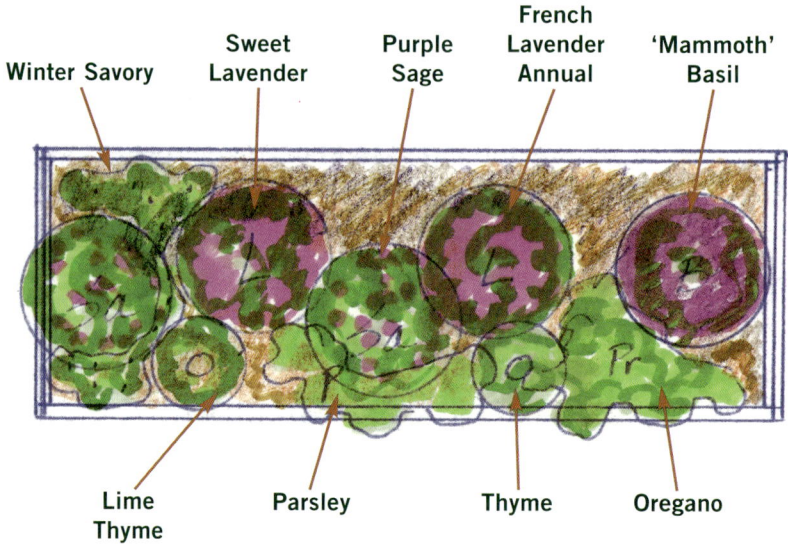

WINDOWBOX HERB GARDEN

What could be better? Your windowbox not only looks beautiful, but produces plants that are good to eat! And because you're providing an almost perfect environment for growth, you have a garden that takes very little work.

BENEFITS / A windowbox provides good drainage, which herbs need. It also gets the plants up into the sunlight, which herbs also need. It keeps bees (herbs attract bees) away from the walkways and you'll have fewer weeds, insects and diseases.

STRUCTURE / A windowbox herb garden can actually be planted in any kind of container as long as it is in the sun (most herbs need at least some sun to grow). The container should be 12" to 18" deep, with good drainage.

You can design and grow your herb garden based on a theme. Grow a windowbox of herbs that are good for making salsa. Or grow herbs for Italian cooking. A garden with herbs for grilling can be especially pretty, as well as tasty. Of course, you can also grow a mix of all kinds of herbs.

Make sure the tallest plants are in back so they don't block the sun from the shorter plants. Sages will get quite large after the first year and will require pruning.

SOIL AND SOIL AMENDMENTS / Buy a professional potting mix for containers at your garden center.

FERTILIZER / You will need to fertilize periodically. Add a small amount of compost to the windowbox once or twice each growing season. Do not over-fertilize.

WATERING / The easiest way is to hand water at the base of the plants.

BORDER FLOWER GARDEN

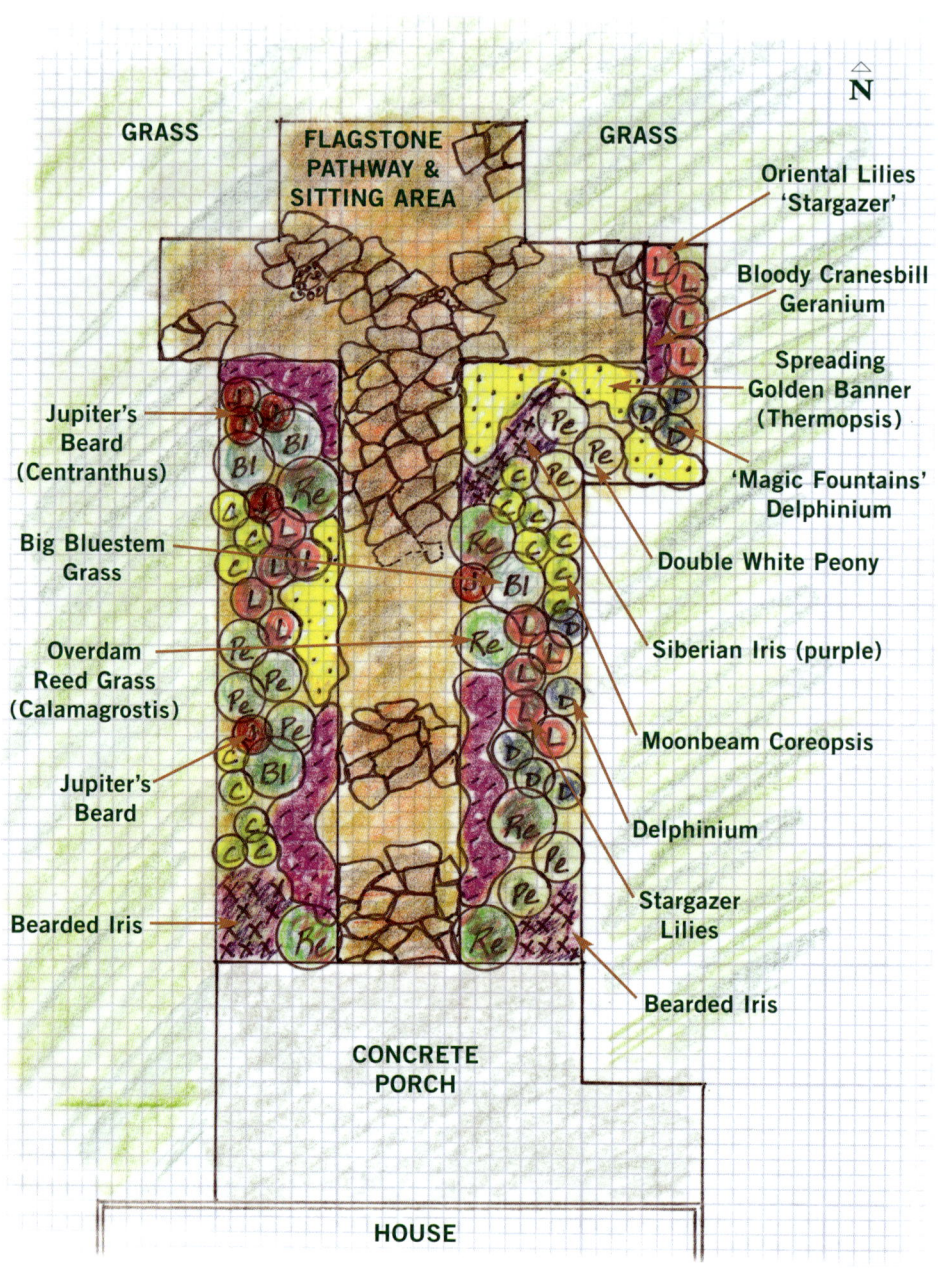

BORDER FLOWER GARDEN

Perennials and annuals dance together in a border flower garden to delight the senses like nothing. Perennials create the backbone of your garden. They can be sophisticated or simple, orderly or boisterous, flashy or subdued. Annuals dart here and there, brilliant in their colors, showing off for their one season of life.

STRUCTURE / You could plant only annuals, but what an investment of time and money every single year! Your perennials are those faithful friends who will, with a minimal amount of maintenance, show up in your garden beds beginning each March (and as late as November in some microclimates). Annuals, on the other hand, give you the chance to experiment and add variety each year.

A border flower garden is generally viewed from one side. Don't place tall plants in front of the shorter ones because they obscure the viewing of the smaller plants. This garden can be designed formally or informally. An informal garden tends to have more random heights, an asymmetrical design and grouped plants. In a formal garden, the flowers are systematically balanced and are usually planted in rows with a more precise gradation in height.

The key is to match both perennials and annuals to your particular microclimate. Choose those that work with your existing landscape. Keep in mind that the lighting in Colorado is different than in other parts of the United States. Because of the bright sunlight, we need brighter plant colors – the softer colors can appear washed out here. Start by choosing plants for their variety in foliage color and texture, then consider bloom color. This will provide a display that is attractive even when plants are between blooms.

Vary the theme. Have an all-purple border flower garden. Or plant a moon garden using white flowers that are highlighted by moonlight. Try a fragrant garden, choosing plants that are the same height (as in the design), but substitute flowers with fragrance. (The garden pictured here features perennials, but you can add your favorite annuals to compliment this design.)

INSECTS AND DISEASES / Maintaining a balance between insect pests and beneficial insects in the garden is important. Simple treatments (*see page 129*) will usually suffice to take care of flower pests and diseases if the helpful insects can't do the job on their own.

A Special Note / The traditional plants that comprise an English garden are very difficult to keep healthy here. However, you can substitute plants that will bring out the essence of this type of setting. The feel of your garden comes as much from form, texture and layout as it does from the actual flowers.

INTERIOR GARDEN

INTERIOR GARDEN

Indoor container gardening is about simplicity. You can design your garden to fit any space. If a plant outgrows its location, simply put it in another spot. Diseased or infested plants can be moved, treated and returned when healthy. Best of all, you're free to experiment with colors, heights, textures – just move the containers around!

BENEFITS / Plants help clean the air. Did you know that one mother-in-law's tongue plant will significantly clean the air in a 10' x 10' room in 24 hours (any 3' tall plant will work). The other benefit to growing plants indoors is aesthetics. Plants look great. They create balance and harmony. The result is that they make you feel good.

STRUCTURE / The considerations about which plants to purchase are much like the considerations for outdoor gardening. How much light does the plant need? (The sun is very intense here, so don't place any plant in the direct sunlight for a number of hours.) How large will it get? What textures and colors do you like best? Is the plant fairly disease-resistant? How much maintenance does it require? Are you willing and able to give the time? These things determine the structure of your interior garden of plants.

SOIL AND SOIL AMENDMENTS / All-purpose potting soil with a Canadian peat base is highly recommended. An all-purpose fertilizer with a 13-13-13 breakdown should work just fine. Fertilize just once, maybe twice a year – more often can be harmful (although many gardeners like to fertilize regularly with a liquid fertilizer as long as the plant is actively growing).

WATERING / The biggest fallacy is that you're supposed to let interior plants dry out between waterings – not true. Most problems with houseplants are caused by underwatering, not overwatering. If you are overwatering, you'll know it because the plants stand in water and will give off a musty smell. The soil for indoor plants should be damp at all times. (Some plants do like to dry out between waterings, so check the requirements for each plant.)

A Special Note / Grow a variety of plants in your home! Try orchids near your east-facing windows, for instance (start simply with a moth orchid and work your way up). Grow herbs in a south-facing window, or put a mother-in-law's tongue in a north-facing location.

MOUNTAIN GARDEN

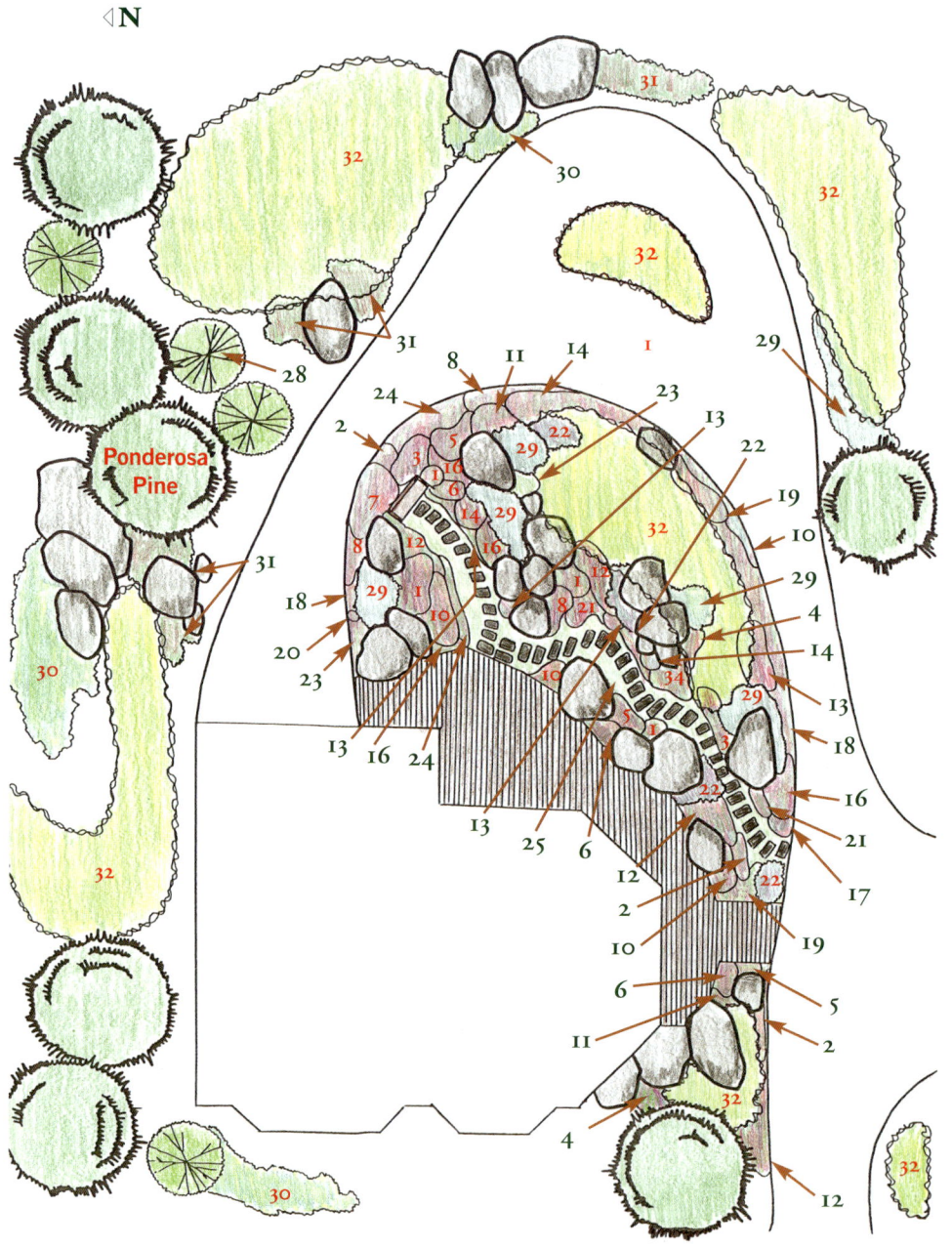

MOUNTAIN GARDEN

KEY

1. False forget-me-not
2. Creeping phlox ("White Delight")
3. Peach leaf harebell, white
4. Lady's mantle
5. Fall aster ("Alert")
6. Snowdrop windflower
7. Salvia ("Mainacht")
8. Columbine (Mix - "Dove")
9. Purple coneflower
10. Geranium ("Kashmir White")
11. Columbine ("Bluejay")
12. Beardstongue
13. Cushion spurge
14. Peach leaf harebell, blue
15. Deadnettle ("Shell Pink")
16. Foxglove ("Excelsior")
    Foxglove ("Mertonensis")
    Foxglove ("Foxy")
    Foxglove ("Purpurea Alba")
17. Harebell ("White Clips")
18. Turkish Veronica
19. Beardstongue ("Rondo")
20. Harebell ("Blue Clips")
21. Geranium ("Johnson's Blue")
22. Daphne ("Rosy Glow")
23. Foxglove ("Grandiflora")
24. Creeping phlox ("Emerald Pink")
25. Vinca minor ("Bowles") Phlox ("Emerald Blue")
26. Creeping phlox ("Emerald Blue")
    Vinca minor ("Bowles")
    Spring bulb collection:
    Narcissus, grape hyacinth, crocus, species tulips, dwarf iris and snowdrops
    Columbine ("Dove" and "Bluejay")
27. Deadnettle ("Shell Pink")
    Geranium ("Johnson's Blue")
    Spring bulb collection:
    Narcissus, grape hyacinth, crocus species tulips, dwarf iris and snowdrops
    Columbine ("Dove" and "Bluejay")
28. Russian hawthorn
29. Peking cotoneaster
30. Thimbleberry
31. Three leaf sumac
32. Aspen

EXISTING
Ponderosa pine

MOUNTAIN GARDEN

In the vast expanse of the Rocky Mountains, there is comfort in defining a niche – a small, private space for yourself.

BENEFITS / The mountains are peaceful, quiet and green. But even the natural beauty of the mountains and forest can be enhanced and complemented by adding colors and textures.

STRUCTURE / Work with, not against, the existing landscape. Use the ponderosa pines to define flow; incorporate outcroppings of moss rock into garden areas; and blend your plants with the native shrubs and flowers that are already growing.

If your area is on a well (which many are), growing your garden at the top of a steep incline may be more difficult. Large expanses of grass or plants that require a lot of water also could pose a problem if the water production is low.

Every part of the country has microclimates. Nowhere are these more apparent than in the mountains. Temperatures can fluctuate as much as 10° between one side of a landscape and another, depending on the wind, slope, grade of land, exposure and the number of trees or amount of shade. Plant materials must be selected based on all these factors, not just plant hardiness guides.

MOUNTAIN GARDEN

SOIL AND SOIL AMENDMENTS / Because of the rocks in the soil, double digging is recommended (*see page 127*) and, if possible, tilling down to a depth of 12". The good news is that if you go to this trouble in the beginning, you will only need to top dress (rake in 2" to 3" of compost) your gardens every two to three years. Unless your trees are diseased, don't rake up the pine needles because, over time, the decomposition will enrich the plants and soil.

INSECTS AND DISEASES / The major insect problems seen in the mountains are mountain pine beetle, white pine weevil and, to a lesser extent, aphids and slugs (*see page 129*). Minimal slug problems can be treated by using a saucer of beer in the garden. Slugs are drawn to beer, fall into the liquid and drown.

WATERING / If your plants are well watered, they will endure winter better. Winter watering, preferably by hand (*see page 124*), is important. (Don't water on top of snow.)

PATIO GARDEN

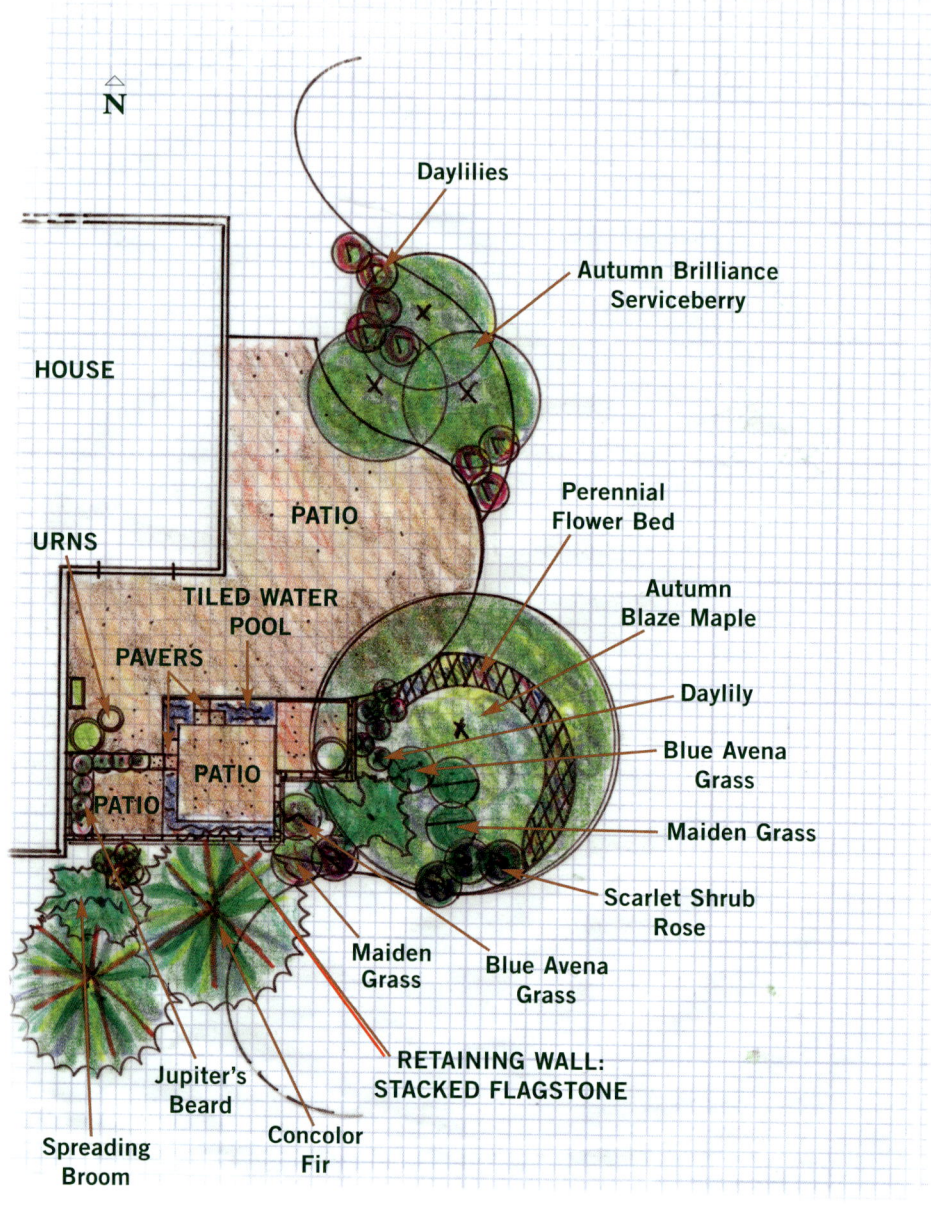

PATIO GARDEN

A patio garden is a commentary on what makes life here so appealing. For at least six months of the year, you will find no better outdoor living. Even in the winter, many days are touched with our warm sun, so you can relax on your patio and enjoy the fresh air, the birds and the sunshine.

BENEFITS / A well-designed and well-constructed patio garden creates an extension of your home that serves to carry your interior ambiance outside and the exterior environment inside. Patio gardens can express your lifestyle. You may prefer a private, intimate setting or you may use your patio for entertaining and socializing. Maybe your patio is one of your children's play areas. Creatively designed, some patios can function as all three. The plantings in your patio garden will be enjoyed in close proximity as you sit and relax, so you should plant some of your favorites. Plant material that is considered less hardy, such as redbuds, Japanese maples and the tender perennials, can be successfully grown around the patio because of protection provided by the house and any enclosure walls.

SPACE AND SIZE / Patios and their gardens come in all shapes and sizes, yet all are formed by available space and the primary functions needed to accommodate your lifestyle. Consider the use of the space. A rule of thumb is that a 12' diameter patio should be the minimum for a 4' round table with chairs.

SITING / Most patio gardens are located at the rear of the residence. This allows the barbecue location to be near the kitchen and also maintains the concept of bringing the outdoors into the residence. Sometimes patio gardens can be located away from the house and in the landscape as a destination seating area.

MATERIAL / The materials chosen will determine the ambiance created and the construction cost. Materials chosen for freestanding and retaining walls should harmonize with the house. A brick Tudor house shouldn't have timber retaining walls – matching brick or red flagstone would be better. Paving materials vary in cost, with gray concrete being the least expensive and mortared buff flagstone being one of the most expensive. Aesthetic considerations are that drylaid brick pavers, stone and wood decks are more casual and, conversely, mortared brick and stone are more formal. If your budget requires a less than "top of the line" paving material, you can upgrade the look of the patio with an outstanding surrounding garden.

PATIO GARDEN

Mortared brick and stone paving set onto a concrete subbase provides a solid and long-lasting patio. However, drylaid patios of brick or cut stone are very durable and sometimes better in areas of expansive soils. The brick or stone can easily be reset if heaving or settling problems occur. And, drylaid patios also are less expensive than the mortared application.

Other considerations for your patio are lighting and shade. Patios are used most often in the afternoon and evening. Shade in the late afternoon and soft lighting will extend the enjoyment of your garden into the late evening hours.

SOIL AND SOIL AMENDMENTS / Amend the existing soil around your patio for the garden as you would for any other garden (*see page 127*). You may want to "double-dig" the areas where you are proposing annuals and perennials. However, the key is to improve your existing soil, not totally replace it, no matter how small the garden is.

INSECTS AND DISEASES / These will be the same as you find on page 129, with some additional considerations. The microclimates created by some patio gardens will cause certain areas to be more susceptible to mites. If you are afraid of bees, avoid plants that bloom when few other plants are blooming. Succulent ground covers and ornamental grasses attract few bees. If you like to watch butterflies, grow plants that attract them (*see page 39*).

WATERING / If you can manage it, drip irrigation is the most effective and efficient watering solution for patio gardens. Pop-up irrigation also should be considered, but the small planting spaces around some patios need to be carefully designed to avoid overspray. The key is not to overwater since this could put stress on the patio structure as well as the plants.

A Special Note / When selecting the plant materials for your patio space, the overriding factor is that you will be in close proximity to the plantings. Texture, color, fragrance and size are the most important considerations. Fine-textured plants usually are better than coarse-textured plants; flowers can be subdued as well as bright. It's good to have some white flowers for night enjoyment. In most residential patio gardens, the smaller dwarf varieties of plants are the best choice.

HOW-TO TIPS

HOW-TO TIPS

HOW TO CLEAN INDOOR CONTAINER PLANTS /
The best way to thoroughly clean houseplants is to take them outdoors. The temperature must be 60° or warmer, but never place the plants in the full sun because the leaves will burn in as little as 10 minutes. To keep the soil intact and in the pots, ball up newspapers on top of the soil and put them around the base of the plant. (This also keeps bugs and dust that are cleaned off the leaves from falling in the soil.) Lay the pot on its side and spray the plant down with the garden hose. Then take a soapy water solution (1 ounce of mild dishwashing detergent (like Ivory) mixed with 23 ounces of water) and spray the plant thoroughly. Let the solution sit on the plant for three to five minutes, then spray it down thoroughly with the garden hose. If your plants are infested with spider mites or scale, repeat this process three weeks in a row. Let the plant dry out for several minutes in the shade and then bring it inside.

HOW TO COMPOST /
What is compost? It's organic matter you can use to supplement and fertilize your soil. It's full of tiny microorganisms that help provide important nutrients for your plants. It also helps break up the clay or hold moisture in sandy or rocky soil. You don't have to add compost to your soil, but your plants will grow much better if you do. The idea is to mix together things like grass clippings from lawns that have not been chemically treated, fallen leaves, pine needles, small wood chips, discarded plant materials, coffee grounds and vegetable and fruit refuse. Let them decompose together. You then add a small amount of this decomposed material or "compost," to the soil around your plants.

There are lots of ways to make compost. One of the easiest methods is to simply make a pile in a corner in your backyard. Keep in mind that the compost tends to attract neighborhood pets and, if not tended properly, it may smell bad. If you want to compost and you live in an urban environment, you can buy several different kinds of black plastic compost bins. There are three things you need to remember to do while composting: (1) chop up any materials going into the bin so they decompose more quickly; (2) turn the pile once a week to aid microorganisms in the decomposition process; and (3) keep the compost pile damp (not soggy!). Plant material won't decompose to form compost if the materials in the bin are too dry. Don't put animal or human waste, meat or weeds full of seed heads in the compost bin.

HOW-TO TIPS

HOW TO DEADHEAD /

It's important to get rid of flower blossoms just after they have died, especially on those plants that repeat-flower. Deadheading annuals and perennials leads to more blossoms, healthier plants the next year and a better looking garden.

Pinch off the individual blooms on flowers that cluster, like petunias. On flowers that grow on single leafy stems, such as daisies, cut back to just above the top growing leaves. For flowers that grow on plants such as daylilies, cut the flower back as far down as you can after it has bloomed. The stems of roses that have bloomed should be cut back at an upward slant up to where the stem is as thick as a pencil and ¼" above a leaflet. (It is generally recommended that you make your cut above a five or seven leaflet for good bloom and to allow enough strength to support the flower. Cutting back to a three leaflet often is not strong enough for good bloom.) Seal off rose stems with a dab of white household glue or commercial rose solvent.

HOW TO KEEP THE DEER AND ELK AWAY /

Start by growing plants around the outside of your garden that deer and elk don't like: iris, yarrow, globe thistles, sagebrush, lavender, chives, ornamental onions, garlic chives, yucca and mountain mahogany. (Deer and elk like coneflower, peonies, hollyhocks, impatiens, crocus, daylilies, sedum, phlox, rhododendrons, roses and tulips.) You also can structure your garden to "flow" around existing deer or elk traffic. Some people hang bars of soap from string (two or three bars to a tree) as a deer repellent. There are also deer repellents that can work, but these often need to be reapplied after every rain or snow. Of course, electric fences or specially designed elk or deer fences are the best solution.

HOW-TO TIPS

HOW TO DEEP WATER

Trees and shrubs should be deep watered during every season here (unless the ground is frozen), especially during the first two years after they are planted. Roses, perennials and lawns also should be deep watered as needed. (*For minimum penetration depths for your plants and lawn, check How-To Water on page 124.*) This means you need to apply water around root zones at least once a month (if the soil is not frozen), on a warm day (above 40°). Water early in the day so the water will soak in before night.

One method of deep watering trees and shrubs is to use a root feeder or a soil needle, which attaches to your garden hose. The feeder should be inserted about 8" into the soil. With new trees or shrubs, you need to water from the trunk to the "drip line" (directly below where the longest branch extends out). With more established plants, water further out, beyond the drip line. (It won't help to water near the trunk.) Holes should be approximately one foot apart. Angle the feeder down and away from the trunk, turn the water on to a medium level and run in each hole for about 30 seconds.

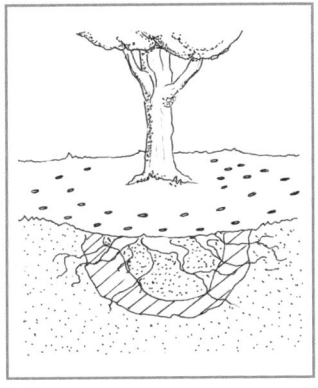

For lawns, garden beds, roses and landscapes with heavy clay soil (or if you just don't want to use a deep root water needle), surface-watering is recommended. Water once a month during the winter and many times a month during the hottest summer months. Simply move the hose around the drip line of the tree or shrub for approximately 15 to 20 minutes, or around various locations in your garden for 30 to 45 minutes. Watch for water pooling. This may indicate that the ground is saturated or the drainage is poor. (Most plants do not grow well in saturated, soggy soil, so reduce watering in these areas and improve soil drainage.) Don't forget to maintain 1" to 3" of mulch on your landscape all year long to conserve and retain moisture.

HOW-TO TIPS

HOW TO FERTILIZE /

If you amend your soil every year and water properly, most of your plants, including most perennials, annuals, bulbs and vegetables, will not need additional fertilizer. If you think your plants need fertilizing, however, add a well-balanced organic or inorganic fertilizer. (Do not apply a balanced fertilizer in any area three years in a row.) While our soil does need more nitrogen, too much will encourage weeds and weak plant growth. Fertilizers are sold with a label that indicates the levels of nitrogen, phosphate (phosphorus) and potash (potassium). For example, a fertilizer that reads 5-10-5 on the front of the bag contains 5% nitrogen, 10% phosphorus and 5% potassium.

You don't necessarily have to fertilize established trees and shrubs, and those that are newly planted or transplanted will benefit from only a little extra feeding. Good fertilizers are those that are slow release. This means the tree or shrub will be able to use the fertilizer needed.* Feed trees through a deep feeder (*see How-To Tip on page 113*) or by pellet fertilizer sprinkled near it.

For roses, there are organic fertilizers containing alfalfa meal, bone meal, sulfur and iron. Roses will also thrive with a commercial fertilizer containing equal amounts of nitrogen and potash, and more phosphate. This mix helps promote root growth and blooming potential. A good mix would read "5-10-5" on the label. After removing any mulch, sprinkle fertilizer on top of the soil around the base of the bush, then rake it in and water deeply. Fertilize your rose bushes once a month during the growing season, but no later than mid-August.

Lawn grass, particularly Kentucky bluegrass, likes lots of nitrogen. When purchasing a commercial fertilizer, look for a high content of nitrogen, half as much phosphate and then half again as much potash (20-10-5 on the label). Also, make sure there is a small amount of iron and about 10% to 15% sulfur. If using organic fertilizer, look for a slow-release fertilizer.* Buffalograss needs very little fertilizer, so one application of nitrogen in the fall should suffice.

* Slow-release fertilizers don't work well in the mountains (except for indoor plants). Instead, use a liquid soluble or foliar feed fertilizer.

HOW-TO TIPS

Fertilize your houseplants once a year with a time-release fertilizer that breaks down over nine months (over-fertilizing houseplants can do more harm than good). The plant will utilize the fertilizer when it needs it most, in the late spring and summer, rather than during the winter. Look for a fertilizer that is labeled 13-13-13 (nitrogen, phosphate, potash). Use a soluble fertilizer when the plant is actively growing.

HOW TO MULCH /

Mulch is organic or inorganic matter that is placed on the ground around plants, trees and shrubs. Mulch moderates soil temperatures, controls weeds, helps the soil retain moisture and keeps the landscape looking neat and trim. Mulches that can be used here include gravel, wood chips, shredded bark, pine needles and straw. Grass clippings or leaves can be used, but be sure they are disease- and insect-free. Old newspapers (or cardboard) also make a good mulch in vegetable and perennial gardens. Spread the newspaper around plants and everywhere that you want nothing to grow. Then cover it with a thin layer of wood chips, bark, etc. Breathable landscape fabric also works well, especially as a weed barrier, but it needs to be covered with either organic or inorganic material. Leave a few inches between the plants, trees and shrubs and the mulch. November is a good time to mulch your perennial beds to help the soil retain badly needed moisture through the winter and to prevent the soil from heaving due to temperature fluctuations. A good time to mulch annual beds is at the time of planting, again, to help the soil retain moisture and to provide a weed barrier.

HOW-TO TIPS

HOW TO HARVEST COMMON VEGETABLES FROM THE KITCHEN GARDEN /

COOL-SEASON VEGETABLES

Broccoli	Cut the flowers (which are the heads) off before hot weather comes, because they will open and become bitter and inedible.
Brussel sprouts	Pick when they are approximately 1" in diameter and green in color. Remove from the plant beginning with the sprouts at the bottom first.
Carrots	Look for shoulders (the top part of the vegetable protruding from the soil) that are 1" across and orange in color.
Lettuce	Cut at the base of the plant near the ground when the leaves are big enough to put in salads (7" to 8" long and 4" to 5" wide, depending on the variety).
Onions	Pull them when most of the tops have fallen over. Before using, put them in a sunny, dry spot for one week.
Peas	Pick when peas are 3" to 4" in length, bright green in color and firm in texture.
Potatoes	Harvest potatoes when blossoms appear – usually about 7 to 8 weeks after they have been planted. Dig carefully around the plant and remove the larger potatoes, leaving the smaller to continue to grow. (Start digging about 1 foot away from the plant and "tunnel" in to minimize damage to the potato.)
Spinach	Harvest similar to lettuce or pull off outer leaves periodically for salads.

HOW-TO TIPS

HOW TO HARVEST COMMON VEGETABLES FROM THE KITCHEN GARDEN /

MAIN-SEASON OR HOT-SEASON VEGETABLES

Chiles	Pick the pod with the stem attached (allow for longer stems when making ristras). (*See page 46.*) Chiles can be picked green or red. Green chile is immature and if left on the plant will turn red. If picked, green chile will shrivel and not turn a bright red color. Red chile is normally picked for winter use.
Cucumbers	Pick before they grow beyond 7" for most varieties. Shriveled and yellow cucumbers, which taste bitter, may be due to under-watering when fruit was forming. Harvest before a hard frost.
Garlic	Pick when the plant tops are dry. Pull out the entire plant, braid the tops together and hang in a dry area for winter use.
Herbs	The best time to pick herbs is in the morning, about 10 a.m. (You want to wait until the herbs are dry, so you don't crush them in the picking.) The leaves of herbs can be cut and used fresh at any time during the season. If you want to use the herbs later, either freeze them immediately (no moisture, in air-tight bags) or dry them out. (*See page 54.*) If you plan to use them later, harvest them when the plants begin to flower.
Pole beans	Pick beans off vines before they are full if you want to eat them entirely. If growing for seeds or "beans," let the the fruit mature. Harvest before a hard frost.
Peppers	Pick when the pepper is at least 3" across and color is a deep green (or purple, yellow or red). Harvest before a hard frost.
Radishes	Look for shoulders (the top part of the vegetable protruding from the soil) that are at least ½" across. Pull up gently. Wash off soil before storing in refrigerator. Radishes can be ready to harvest 4 to 6 weeks after planting, so watch these carefully.
Tomatoes	Pick when fruit turns a deep, rich red color. For best flavor, try to leave on the vine to ripen. When an early frost is predicted, pick green tomatoes and let ripen indoors in indirect light.
Tomatillos	Pick when the papery skin around the fruit drys out.
Zucchini	A type of summer squash. Harvest when 6" long. Zucchini that grows large often tastes very bland and sometimes bitter. Harvest zucchini before a hard frost.

HOW-TO TIPS

HOW TO PLANT OR TRANSPLANT ROSE BUSHES

Choose a sunny site. Make sure the soil has been properly prepared (*see How-To Tip on page 127*), then dig a hole deep enough to plant even with the graft (or with the graft 2" below the ground at higher elevations). (The graft is a knobby area just above the roots and at the bottom of the limbs.) With bare-root or transplanted bushes, try to spread the roots out to encourage stronger root growth. Using soil, you can form a cone in the bottom of the hole to place the roots around (like a tepee). With container bushes, take the bush out of the pot and make sure to remove wires or plastic wraps before you plant. Place the bush in the hole and backfill with amended soil. Mix in a thin layer of triple super-phosphate with the soil in the bottom of the hole before planting. Soak the planted area thoroughly. Plant hybrid tea roses 2' to 2½' apart; miniature roses 1' to 1½' apart; groundcover roses 3' apart; and bush and shrub roses 4' apart.

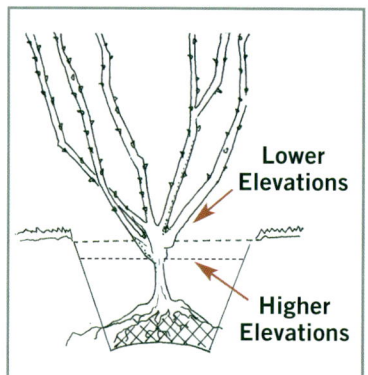

HOW-TO TIPS

HOW TO PRUNE /
There are several reasons to prune your trees and shrubs. Pruning removes dead and diseased branches, encourages a healthier plant, inspires more fruitful production and prevents the spread of disease and insects. To a much lesser degree, careful pruning gives the tree or shrub an improved shape.

DECIDUOUS TREES / Near the place where the trunk and the branch meet is a slight mound of bark called the collar. When you prune, cut at an angle, outside the collar. If you cut inside the collar, the wound takes longer to heal, allowing disease and insects to get into the trunk. If you can't find a collar, make a cut at a right angle going outward from the trunk. Do not leave long stubs on the tree. Avoid cutting off main trunk limbs, but if they are diseased or already dead, prune back.

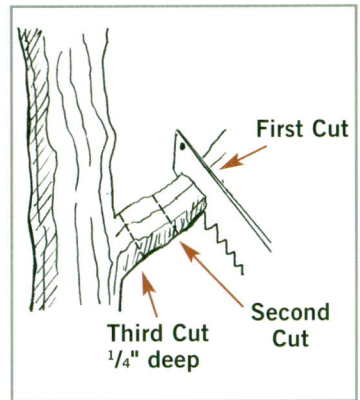

DECIDUOUS SHRUBS / If the canes are diseased or are producing weak, leggy foliage, prune the oldest and weakest canes at or near the ground. If you want trimmer, less dense plants, remove one-third of the oldest canes at the base of the plant, near the ground. Do not shear your shrubs (trimming off the top of the branches) because this causes excessive growth at the tip of the branches, which will shade out inside leaf growth (this could lead to unhealthy and diseased shrubs). Prune spring-flowering shrubs after they bloom, not in the winter.

Evergreen trees and shrubs don't need much pruning at all. In fact, keep in mind that evergreens that are cut back excessively may not grow back. If you want to control the growth of a few branches, snip the candles part way (yellow/brown growth that shoots out from the end of the branches).

HOW-TO TIPS

HOW TO CREATE A MINIATURE ORCHARD IN YOUR BACKYARD /

You can have a small orchard in your backyard, even if you have limited space. Plant two or more different fruit trees in the same hole, 18" apart. You can plant dwarf, semi-dwarf or standard fruit trees. The benefits of close planting, besides saving space, are that the trees won't grow as big because they are competing (good pruning is a must!) and there is better cross-pollination with some varieties. The trees will still produce a nice amount of fruit, however.

HOW TO PLANT AND TRANSPLANT TREES AND SHRUBS /

For bare-root trees and shrubs, dig the hole wide enough to spread the roots out (they shouldn't curve up the sides of the hole) and deep enough that the place where the roots and the trunk meet will be at the same level it was when growing in the nursery. (In lower elevations, plant even with the ground; at higher elevations, 2" to 3" above the ground so the soil can settle.) Take two-thirds of the soil from the hole and mix it (amend) with one-third organic matter such as compost or peat moss. Shovel the amended soil around the tree until it is filled to the top of the hole. (Do not pack the soil down.) Create a mound of dirt around the outside edge of the hole, fill it with water and let the water soak into the ground. Then water as needed. (*See How-To Tip on page 124.*) Put 2" to 3" of mulch (*see How-To Tip on page 115*) around the plant.

For balled and burlapped trees and shrubs, dig the hole twice as wide as the ball and deep enough that the ball will be at the same level that it was growing in the nursery. (In lower elevations, plant even with the ground; at higher elevations, 2" to 3" above the ground, so the soil can settle.) Take two-thirds of the soil from the hole and mix it (amend) with one-third organic matter, such as compost or peat moss. It is very important to remove the wire or twine from the ball before it is planted and also remove the top third of the wire basket after the plant is placed in the hole.

HOW-TO TIPS

Cut the burlap back slightly from the tree or shrub and tuck it down around the root so it does not act like a wick (remove synthetic wrap – it will not decompose). Remove all twine from around the trunk and the ball. If the ball is wrapped with shrink-wrap, remove it. Shovel amended soil around the tree until it is filled to the top of the hole (do not pack the soil down). Create a mound of dirt around the edge of the hole, fill it with water and let the water soak into the ground. Then water as needed. (*See How-To Tip on page 124*.) Put 5" of mulch (*see How-To Tip on page 115*) around the plant.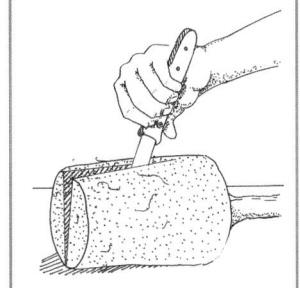

For container trees and shrubs (except pines), follow the same directions as above for balled and burlapped plants, except do the following – take the plant out of the container carefully (make sure the soil is damp, not dry, to make this easier). If the roots appear matted around the sides, or if they circle the bottom, try to loosen and pull them away from the sides of the root ball.

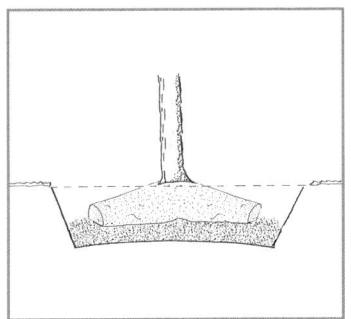

For pines, or if you can't pull the roots away by hand, cut down the sides ½" in three to four places with a knife or gardening spade. If the roots are all down at the bottom of the ball, take an axe, shovel or sharp knife and, from the middle of the bottom, cut a little less than halfway up the middle of the root ball. Spread each half out to each side forming a "butterfly." (The plant will actually grow better by loosening or cutting the roots.) Place the butterflied plant on a small mound of soil in the bottom of the hole.

When transplanting, you have to make sure you dig enough of the root system to allow the tree or shrub to reestablish itself quickly in the new location. The American Nurseryman Standards chart suggests how big the root ball should be dug for the type of tree or shrub you want to transplant. Then, follow the directions for planting balled and burlapped trees and shrubs. Transplanting trees and shrubs here in the fall or the middle of summer is risky.

HOW-TO TIPS

HOW TO STAKE TREES /

Some newly planted trees should be staked so they can establish roots. There are several pieces of hardware you must have to stake plants. The stake itself should be at least 2" wide and long enough to go down at least as deep as the bottom of the ball. The stake often is made of metal for durability. The cable that attaches the tree to the stake is called a guy wire. The wire should be attached to tree straps (made with grommets), which wrap around the trunk. Two or three stakes per tree should be enough. Don't stake the tree so tightly that the trunk can't move slightly. A little trunk movement is necessary to stimulate root growth. Make sure the bark is not being rubbed or damaged. Stake the tree only temporarily. If you have a tree that tends to tip over (spruces have a limited root system so they are especially susceptible to snow, wind, overwatering and underwatering), then continue to stake, but move the tree straps around every few months so they are not on the same place on the trunk. Immediately after you stake, do any necessary pruning (the top one-third of the branches on bare-root trees, but do not trim the "leader" or branch that stands tallest). Water newly planted trees regularly for the first five weeks (check your soil for dryness) (*see How-To on page 124*), then as required by the type of tree and the location.

HOW-TO TIPS

HOW TO WEED

There are two types of weeds: perennial (come back every year) and annual (live one year and set seed at the end of the season). Some of the most prevalent perennial weeds in our state are thistle, bindweed and dandelions. Annual weeds include spurge, crabgrass, puncturevine, purslane, knotweed and common chickweed. You can use weed barrier cloth to help keep weeds to a minimum in large areas. After putting the cloth down, cover with a mulch like wood chips or straw. For planting, cut holes in the cloth that are a little wider than the plant. If you use this weeding technique, remember that seeds will have to be planted only in the areas where you cut holes. In smaller areas, you can use several layers of newspaper to achieve the same thing as weed barrier cloth. If you dig or rototill the area first, try not to do it when weeds are just getting ready to reseed (after they bloom), make sure to get the weed roots and mulch immediately. Remove the seedheads – do not till them into the soil! If weeding by hand (for weeds that are growing in and around established plants), either pull them when the soil is damp (to get the entire root) or cut them off at the base with pruners every couple of days until the weed no longer grows. Finally, you can spray weeds with a product that contains the chemical glyphosate (it breaks down in the soil). Be careful with glyphosate – it will kill any plant it contacts. In all cases, weed once a week to keep things under control and spread mulch liberally (*see How-To Tip on page 115*).

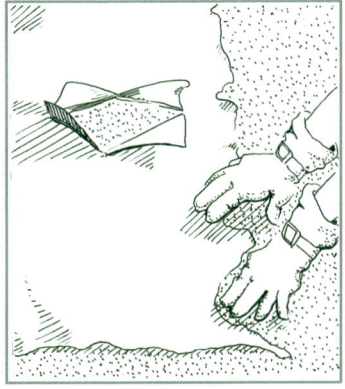

HOW-TO TIPS

HOW TO WATER

The climate in Colorado is highly varied, ranging from mountainous to semi-arid to arid. Overall, however, we don't get a lot of moisture. This means we have to help Mother Nature and water our lawns, gardens, trees, shrubs and, of course, indoor plants.

Some overall suggestions: Be conservative and don't waste water – we don't have a lot to spare. The best time to water is early in the morning. Amending your soil makes it use the water it is given more efficiently. (*See How-To Tip on page 127*.) Mulch your gardens to help them hold moisture. (*See How-To Tip on page 115*.) As a general rule, clay soil absorbs about ½" of water per hour. Sandy and rocky soil absorbs water much faster, so water more frequently for a shorter duration. Until you understand your particular soil, periodically check moisture levels with your finger. Otherwise, there is a tendency to overwater, which causes oxygen starvation in roots and the plant rots in the soil. The dying plant often looks the same as a plant that is drought-stressed.

Generally, the rule on watering is infrequent, slow, deep watering for all plant material. However, you will need to increase the frequency of watering during hot periods and reduce the frequency during winter dormant months.

HOW-TO TIPS

PLANT	HOW TO WATER
Lawn	Kentucky bluegrass needs 24" to 30" of water per year. As a general rule, water 1+" per week during the 20 prime growing weeks of the year (mid-spring to mid-fall). Water long enough for the lawn to collect 1" of water. To test how much water your lawn is getting, set out plastic containers in several areas, turn on the sprinklers and see how long it takes for 1" of water to collect in the container. Periodically test by inserting a screwdriver into the ground in several locations. If the soil isn't damp 6" to 8" down, increase the water; if it's too wet, decrease the water. Lawns need water when footprints show on the lawn and/or the lawn turns a darker purple-blue color. Do not start watering too early in the season as it could lead to an increase in diseases.
Perennial Flowers Annual Flowers and Bulbs	Start by clustering plants with similar watering requirements in beds. (Look at the label on the plant when you buy it.) The best way to water in summer is with a drip-emitter system or a soaker hose at the base of the plants. Transplants can be watered frequently, lightly. Larger, more developed plants need to be soaked thoroughly, which means soil should be damp at least 4" to 6" down. To test, periodically dig down 6" in various parts of your garden to see whether the soil is damp. Increase or decrease water as needed. In either case, make sure the soil has been properly amended. In winter, on a warm day (above 50°), water beds that don't have snow on them. Do this about once a month.
Trees and Shrubs	If trees and shrubs are planted in the lawn, chances are they are getting enough water. Test as you would for the lawn. Thoroughly water new or transplanted trees and shrubs when first planted so the soil will settle. Water every 7 to 10 days during late spring through early fall the first year. Newly planted trees may need watering every third day in hot summer temperatures, depending on the soil type. Water with drip-emitters or hose. Deep water during winter months (*see page 113*) for the first two winters if the ground is not frozen. After the first 1½ to 2 years, trees should be well-enough established so that no additional watering is needed. Some shrubs may need additional watering, so check them all periodically.

HOW-TO TIPS

PLANT	HOW TO WATER
Roses	Water a minimum of 1" per week during the growing season. Water heavily every three days, rather than lightly every day. Thoroughly water new or transplanted roses when first planted so the soil will settle. The best way to water is with a drip-emitter system or with a soaker hose at the base of the roses. To test, periodically dig down 4" to 6" in your rose beds to see whether the soil is damp. Water in winter as needed.
Drought-Tolerant Gardens	If you use native plant materials or buffalograss in your landscape, you can halve the amounts of water listed above. Watering for the first two years, while plants are getting established, still is recommended.
Kitchen Gardens	After planting seeds, water daily with a hand-held hose or water wand. After seedlings appear, water every day in sandy soil and every other day in loamy or clay soil. Water enough to keep the soil damp about 6" to 8" deep. During hot summer months, water gardens daily. Test by digging down 8" in your garden to see whether the soil is damp. Vegetables that receive irregular or limited watering can be bitter tasting. Tomatoes are particularly sensitive and may develop blossom-end rot if growth occurs under irregular watering conditions.
Interior Plants	Most foliage and flowering houseplants should be watered once a week and the soil kept evenly moist. There are exceptions, such as cacti, succulents, bromeliads, etc. (Consult your garden center or nursery.) Do not let the soil dry out between waterings. To start, water your plant and come back in four hours. If there is no water in the saucer, water again. In high-light environments, there should be enough standing water in the saucer that the plant can gradually use it for the next two to three days. (The saucer will then be empty.) In low light, there should be enough standing water in the saucer that the plant uses it in one day. Do not mist your plants – it creates false expectations.

HOW-TO TIPS

HOW TO AMEND COLORADO SOIL

Colorado soil is not as garden-friendly as soil in other states. To begin with, our soils have a high pH. This is a problem because nutrients needed for growth are bound up in the soil. In addition, Colorado soil is either too compact (clay), or not compact enough (rocky or sandy). Clay soils have a tendency to compact, preventing oxygen from getting to the roots. They also hold water. Sandy soils, on the other hand, do not hold water and leach valuable nutrients from the soil. The result, in either case, is that many gardening plants may not be healthy. (There are exceptions to this, especially with native "drought-tolerant" plants.)

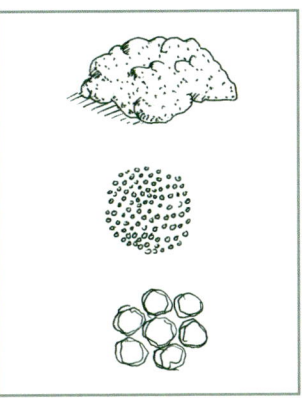

So Colorado soil must be amended. In all cases, the amending is the same, but the goals are different. With clay, the goal is to add materials that will loosen up or get air into the soil and lower the pH. With sandy or rocky soil, the goal is to add materials that will cause the soil to retain water and nutrients. The first question is what type of soil do you have in your landscape? Grab a small handful of damp soil and squeeze it. If the soil feels a little sticky and forms a ball, you have clay soil. If it breaks apart into small pieces and feels rather gritty, you have sandy soil. If the soil contains pieces of rock or small rocks, you have rocky soil.

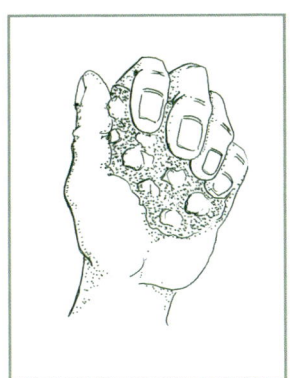

HOW-TO TIPS

To improve Colorado soil, add organic soil amendments like compost (*see How-To Tip on page 111*), or barnyard manure that is at least one year old. (Never use stockyard manure (it contains too much salt) or mountain peat (it's too fine to use as a soil amendment).) The general rule is to add one-third organic material to two-thirds existing soil, or three cubic yards per 1,000 square feet each year. (This is about 1¼" of material on top of the ground.) You must till the organic material into the soil, at least 6" to 8" deep, and up to 12" for really healthy soil. Till when the soil is damp, not wet or dry. If it sticks to the shovel, the soil is too wet. (It's difficult to use a tiller in mountain soil because rocks can break the tines. Instead use either heavy equipment or hand dig your soil.)

HOW-TO TIPS

COLORADO INSECTS AND DISEASES

INSECT OR DISEASE	HOW TO IDENTIFY	WHAT TO DO
Aphids	Tiny, pear-shaped insects; grow in clusters on leaves; emit sticky substance; cause yellowed, withered or curled leaves.	Outdoor plants: spray hard with water every few days for 2 weeks. Use insecticidal soap. Indoor plants: Alcohol wash using 70% rubbing alcohol straight (no water), spray on infected plant leaves (test 1 leaf on each plant first for 3 days), wait 10 minutes, then wash off aphids with water. (The alcohol forces them to "let go," so it's important to then wash them completely off with water.)
Fungus Gnats	Tiny gnats that fly around; usually attack indoor plants.	Remove all debris from the plant – dead leaves, etc. Make sure plant isn't overwatered. Use insect strips (yellow sticky paper) – gnats are attracted to the color yellow.
Lawn Insects and Diseases		Bacillus thuringiensis (Bt)* works for many lawn insects. Check with lawn care experts or extension service for identification and current recommendations for insects and diseases. *(See Lawn Maintenance Calendar on page 150.)*
Mealy Bugs	Bugs that look like little white cotton beads clustered in groups.	Use insecticidal soap. Soap wash (see Spider Mites). Alcohol wash for indoor plants (see Aphids).

*Bacillus thuringiensis (Bt) is an organic microbial insecticide that kills many garden insects. It is nontoxic to mammals and, for the most part, won't harm beneficial insects (do not use it near butterfly caterpillars!). There are various strains of Bt that are pest specific. Read the label for what pests each strain will attack.

HOW-TO TIPS

COLORADO INSECTS AND DISEASES

INSECT OR DISEASE	HOW TO IDENTIFY	WHAT TO DO
Pine Tip Moth	The candles on pine trees stop growing and die. First appears in mid-spring.	Spray with a systemic insecticide.
Powdery Mildew	A fungus that covers leaves and stems with a white powder. Roses are particularly susceptible.	For Powdery Mildew and Black Spot, use light horticultural oil (read label carefully). Baking soda wash: Mix 1 tablespoon baking soda with 1 gallon water. Spray on infected plants. Or mix 1 tablespoon baking soda with 2½ tablespoons light horticultural oil and add to 1 gallon water. (Test 1 leaf on each plant first for 3 days.)
Black Spot	A fungus that causes black spots to appear on the leaves of roses.	
Scale	Small, brown or white bumps with hard covering. They emit a sticky substance.	Use insecticidal soap (only works during crawler stage). Scrape off scale with kitchen scrubbie. Alcohol wash for indoor plants (see Aphids). Dormant oil spray. If nothing works, consult a professional.
Slugs	They have a snail-like appearance without a shell; can be gray or black. They leave a silvery trail of slime wherever they go.	Fill small containers with fresh beer. Place 3' to 4' apart and sink into the ground. Slugs are attracted to beer – they crawl in and drown. Collect by hand after 9 p.m. Keep yard free of trash, old lumber, etc. Place 6" copper screen around garden bed, buried 3" down in the soil (creates an electrical barrier).

HOW-TO TIPS

COLORADO INSECTS AND DISEASES

INSECT OR DISEASE	HOW TO IDENTIFY	WHAT TO DO
Spider Mites	Leaves are mottled with a speckled appearance on the underside of leaves.	Sign of drought stress – check water levels. Use insecticidal soap. Soap wash: mix 1 ounce mild dishwashing detergent (like Ivory) with 23 ounces of warm water and spray on plant, wait 10 minutes, then wash off. Repeat once a week for three weeks. Alcohol wash for indoor plants (see Aphids). Or, simply blast cold water with the hose on the infested plants in the heat of the day.
Tree Diseases	There are over 50 diagnosed diseases and insects that attack trees and shrubs in Colorado.	If preventative measures fail (suitable species for location, properly amended soil, proper watering and maintenance), call tree experts or county extension service for a diagnosis and solution.
Whiteflies	Tiny white insects that can be seen in groups under new leaves of a plant. They like the color yellow.	Use insecticidal soap. Insect strips. Alcohol wash for indoor plants (see Aphids). Nasturtiums (a trap crop for whiteflies).

NOTES

LISTS AND CALENDARS

CHECKLIST

TREES AND SHRUBS IN COLORADO

☐ 1. What is your budget? Trees and shrubs can be very expensive, so it's important to determine how much money you want to spend.

☐ 2. Where in the landscape will the tree be planted? What is the microclimate in which you live and what tree will fit best in the location you have chosen? Will the tree grow well in your microclimate?

☐ 3. What is your lifestyle? What's going to happen in your landscape? Is it just for show? Do you have kids? A dog? What activities take place outside your home – entertainment, sports, gardening?

☐ 4. What is your time-frame from planting to maturity, i.e., how long will you be in your home?

☐ 5. What colors and textures do you like? Plan for colors and textures during all four seasons.

☐ 6. What are your personal likes and dislikes? Do you like fruit? Do you eat berries? Do you make preserves or cook with ingredients from the garden? Do you like dried arrangements?

☐ 7. What are your perceptions of water and watering? Do you have the time to water correctly and properly?

☐ 8. Maintenance: How much time will you spend caring for your trees and shrubs? Do you have local water restrictions?

TREES AND SHRUBS

Trees and shrubs represent the versatility in any landscape. They can be what you want them to be – they are soft, they are strong, they define, they provide diversion. Whatever the setting you want to create, trees and shrubs are important for a landscape that is pleasing to the eye.

BENEFITS / Part of the role that trees and shrubs play in the environment is to reduce pollution. They also add oxygen to the air, as do all plants, through photosynthesis. Trees are coolants, shading other plants, wildlife and people. No other plants provide the depth and variety of color and texture, four seasons of the year, to the Colorado landscape.

TYPE AND STRUCTURE / Expectations are the most important consideration when planting trees and shrubs. Because they are more of an investment than other types of plants, identifying your needs and desires before purchasing is highly recommended. It's difficult to just move a tree after a few years because there was no thought given to where it was planted.

LOCATION IS KEY / Location dictates the kind of soil in an area, the exposure (how much sun and at what times of the day), the amount of water the plant gets and potential diseases. It's also important to note what will be near the tree and what will eventually be growing under the tree. After you've decided where you want to plant a tree or shrub, take some additional time to shop for the best plant for that location. It is very difficult to successfully transplant trees and shrubs in Colorado, so you want to choose a plant that will thrive in the chosen location.

TREES AND SHRUBS

SHOPPING FOR TREES AND SHRUBS – SOME THINGS TO LOOK FOR /
- ☐ Is the soil around the root ball damp (not soaking wet or dry)?
- ☐ Are the trees and shrubs standing upright (not tipped over or lying on their sides)?
- ☐ Are buying from an established nursery/garden center?
- ☐ Is there any browning on deciduous or evergreen trees?
- ☐ Do you know what a fully-grown specimen of what you're buying looks like?
- ☐ Is the tree suitable for the growing zones you live in?
- ☐ Is a warranty offered on the tree or shrub?
- ☐ Is the plant well-rooted?
- ☐ Is it hardened-off for your present weather conditions?
- ☐ Are there any signs of pests on the tree or shrub?

INSECTS AND DISEASES / There are many insects and diseases that can affect trees and shrubs. Some are more life-threatening than others. The key is to continually inspect your trees and shrubs to make sure you catch problems early and then treat them as necessary. A targeted approach is best, taking into consideration the plant species and the insect or disease. If in doubt, ask your garden center or a tree specialist for help!

TREES AND SHRUBS

EVERGREEN TREES AND SHRUBS

UNDER 5' TALL
Oregon grape
Mugo pine
William Penn barberry
Barberry
Yucca baccata

5' TO 20'+ TALL
Austrian pine
Bristlecone pine
Ponderosa pine
Pyracantha
Scotch pine
Yews

20'+ TALL
Austrian pine
Blue spruce
Eastern white pine
Limber pine
Pinon
Rocky Mountain juniper

DECIDUOUS TREES

UP TO 30' TALL
Flowering crabapple
  varieties
Goldenrain
Hawthorns
Linden

30'+ TALL
Ash (green and
  white varieties)
Autumn blaze maple
English oak
Honey locust

30'+ TALL
Western catalpa
Western hackberry

DECIDUOUS SHRUBS

UP TO 4' TALL
Barberry
Blue mist spirea
Chokeberry
Leadplant
Sandcherry

4' TO 10' TALL
Apache plume
Cotoneaster
Currant
Dogwood
Forsythia
Sumac

10'+ TALL
Buffaloberry
Lilac
Cistena plum
Rabbitbrush
Serviceberry
Viburnums

HERBS FOR COLORADO

FOR FRAGRANCE
Artemesia
Chamomile
Eucalyptus
Lavender
Lemon balm
Lemon verbena
Mints
Patchouli
Pineapple sage
Scented geraniums
Valerian

FOR COLOR
African blue basil
Cardinal sage
Cuban oregano
Golden feverfew
Helicryssum
Heliotrope
Miss Jessop rosemary
North's gold oregano
Purple basils
Tricolor sage
Variegated calamint

FOR TALL, FLOWERING SPIKES
Anise hyssop
Baby sage
Echinacea
Fernleaf yarrow
Fruit sage
Lemon balm
Pineapple sage
Russian sage
Valerian

FORMAL GARDENS
Chives
Dwarf hyssop
French thyme
Germander
Lavender
Parsley
Roman chamomile
Rue
Santolina
Winter savory

INFORMAL GARDENS
Comfrey
Feverfew
Hops
Horehound
Lemon verbena
Lemon grass
Mints
Mother of thyme
Mugwort

LARGE HERBS
Angelica
Artemesia
Ashwagandi
Boneset
Butterfly weed
Fennel
Fernleaf dill
French tarragon
Joe-Pye weed
Motherwort
Mugwort
Wormwood

HOT LOCATIONS
Artemesia
Catmint
Chives
Echinacea
Lavender
Oregano
Rosemary
Sage
Santolina
Scented geraniums
Soapwort
Thyme

SHADY LOCATIONS
Angelica
Anise hyssop
Chamomile
Comfrey
Curly wood sage
Chervil
Feverfew
Germander
Ladies mantle
Lungwort
Marjoram
Oregano
Parsley
Sage
Savory
Self heal
Skullcap
Soapwort
Sunset woodruff
Sweet Cicely
Valerian
Wild strawberry
Yerba buena

CONTAINERS IN HOT, SUNNY LOCATIONS
Chamomile
Chives
Lemon thyme
Lemon verbena
Marjoram
Rosemary
Sage
Scented geraniums
Self heal
Tarragon
Winter savory

CONTAINERS IN SHADY LOCATIONS
Bay
Chervil
Gotu kola
Lungwort
Mints
Myrtle
Parsley
Pennyroyal
Salad burnet
Sweet Cicely
Sweet woodruff
Yerba buena

LISTS - 139

XERISCAPE GARDEN
BEST AND WORST LISTS

TREES

BEST	BEST	WORST
Bristlecone pine	Kentucky coffee tree	Aspen
Burr oak	Plum	Beech
Golden rain tree	Pinon pine	Birch
Hackberry	Ponderosa pine	Cottonwood
Hawthorn	Rocky Mountain maple	Magnolia
	Serviceberry	Redbud

SHRUBS

BEST	BEST	WORST
Apache plume	Ninebark	Butterfly bush
Buffaloberry	Peashrub	Deutzia
Cliffrose	Rabbitbrush	Hybrid roses
Cotoneaster	Rock spirea	Hydrangea
Currant	Sagebrush	Mockorange
Gooseberry	Saltbrush	Rhododendron
Juniper	Seabuckthorn	Spirea
Lilac	Shrub roses	St. John's wort
Mountain mahogany	Sumac	Weigela
Leadplant	Yucca	

FLOWERS

BEST	BEST	WORST
Aster	Iris	Astilbe
Blue flax	Jupiter's beard	Bergenia
Baby's breath	Lavender	Black snakeroot
Bearded Iris	Penstemon	Bleeding heart
Columbine	Primrose	Creeping buttercup
Coral bells	Purple coneflower	Euonymous
Coreopsis	Rockcress	Goatsbeard
Creeping phlox	Sage	Hardy ferns
Daisy	Sedum	Hosta
Daylily	Snow-in-summer	Japanese anemone
Dianthus	Sea holly	Japanese spurge
Fleabane	Sun rose	Ligularia
Gaillardia	Torch lily	Meadowsweet
Hardy iceplant	Wild strawberry	Monkshood
		Siberian iris
		Snow-on-the-mountain

MOUNTAIN GARDEN
BEST AND WORST LISTS

BEST

- American plum
- Amur maple
- Aspen
- Autumn joy sedum
- Black locust
- Blue butterfly pincushion flower
- Blue fescue grass
- Bluejay columbine
- Bowels periwinkle
- Bristlecone pine
- Clematis
- Dove columbine
- Douglas fir
- Firecracker penstemon
- Giant flowered penstemon
- Hardy yellow iceplant
- Japanese painted fern
- Karl Foerster feather reed grass
- Limber pine
- Leopard's bane
- Locust
- Lodgepole pine
- May night salvia
- Moonbeam coreopsis (threadleaf)
- Moonshine yarrow
- Narrowleaf cottonwood
- Norway maple
- Peking cotoneaster
- Peter Davis juniper thyme
- Pinon pine (some areas)
- Ponderosa pine
- Prof. Kippenberg fall aster
- Rock soapwort
- Rocky Mountain maple
- Rugosa roses
- Showy evening primrose
- Shrub roses
- Silver sage
- Snowdrops
- Thimbleberry
- Three leaf sumac
- White Clips carpathian bellflower
- Windflower anemone
- Woolly Veronica

WORST

- Apricot trees
- Autumn fern
- Boston ivy
- Broadleaf evergreens
- Buddleia
- Buffalograss
- Carex grasses
- Catalpa
- Ceratostigma
- Colchicum (marginal)
- Forsythia (bloom too early)
- Hibiscus
- Hybrid tea roses
- Ilex
- Linden tree
- Marigolds (marginal)
- Pachysandra
- Pyracantha
- Rose tree of China
- St. John's wort
- Sweetgum tree
- Tree lilac
- Upright juniper (deer food)
- Zinnia grandiflora

PATIO GARDEN
BEST AND WORST LISTS

TREES
Consider size, shading traits, accenting/enclosure and leaf/berry drop.

BEST	BEST	WORST
Character pines	Montmorency cherry	Austrian pine
Dwarf conifers	Serviceberry	Blue spruce
Ginnala maple	Spring snow crabapple	Fruit trees that drop messy fruit
Golden rain tree	Thornless cockspur hawthorne	Russian olive
Japanese tree lilac		

SHRUBS
Consider size, leaf/winter stem texture, flower/leaf color, fragrance and seasonal interest. Most larger shrubs are not suggested except as accent planting.

BEST	BEST	WORST
Anthony Waterer spirea	Dwarf burning bush	Alder
Burkwood viburnum	Kelsi dogwood	Beautybush
Carol Mackie daphne	Low growing junipers	Blue mist spirea
Cistena plum	Rabbitbrush	Common ninebark
Dwarf Korean lilac	Roses	Pfitzer juniper
Dwarf barberry		Pyracantha

PERENNIALS AND GROUND COVERS
These provide the most diversity of plants to consider around the patio garden and are a matter of personal preference. The worst plants are listed primarily because they can be too big, too aggressive, or their texture and size might not fit a patio garden.

BEST SUN	BEST SUN	WORST SUN
Alpine and Icelandic poppies	Dianthus deltoides	Bee balm
Bellflower	Dwarf asters	Delphinium
Columbine	Dwarf ornamental grasses	Large ornamental grass
Coreopsis	Lavender	Snow-in-summer
	Salvia	Yarrow

BEST SHADE	BEST SHADE	WORST SHADE
Astilbe	Hosta	Aegopodium (Bishops Weed)*
Coral bells	Lamium	Anemone (buttercup)*
Dwarf bleeding heart	Oregon grape holly	Moneywort*
Euonymus coloratus	Sweet woodruff	Potentilla verna*
Ferns	Vinca/Periwinkle	

*These ground covers are aggressive and will crowd out a mixed perennial garden. They can be used as a mass planting under shrubs/trees.

INTERIOR GARDEN
/ BEST AND WORST LISTS

BEST

NORTH WINDOWS
Bamboo palm
Cast iron plant
Chinese evergreen (Aglaonema)
Dracaenas (many species)
Kentia palm
Mother-in-law's tongue
Parlor palm
Philodendron

EAST WINDOWS
Dieffenbachia
Dracaenas (many species)
Fiddle leaf fig
Moth orchids
Nephthytis
Philodendron
Strawberry begonia

SOUTH WINDOWS
Cactus
Copperleaf
Dracaenas (many species)
Fiddle leaf fig
Geranium
Lemon tree
Orange tree
Pony tail palm
Rubber plant
Strawberry geranium
Succulents (aloe, jade, donkey's tail)

WEST WINDOWS
Dracaenas (many species)
Ficus trees
Fiddle leaf fig
Philodendron
Succulents

WORST

Baby tears
Birdsnest fern
Boston fern
Calathea (prayer plant family)
Fluffy ruffles fern
Heather
Pineapple bromeliad
Starlite bromeliad

SHADE GARDEN
BEST AND WORST LISTS

BEST

Astilbe
Begonias
Dead nettle
Coleus
Coral bells
Foxglove
Ferns
Hosta
Impatiens

Japanese anemone
Lady's mantle
Leadwort
Lungwort
Nicotiana
Pansy
Periwinkle
Skullcap
Sweet woodruff

WORST

Bubble gum mint (gets leggy)
Cistena plum (loses color)
Daisies (gets leggy)
Delphinium (gets leggy)
English ivy (invasive)

Gaillardia (gets leggy)
Golden privet (loses color)
Obedient plant (invasive)
Potentillas (loses color)

WINTER GARDEN
BEST AND WORST LISTS

BEST

Apache plume (white bark)
Blue avena grass
Blue chip juniper
Broom (moonlight)
Cranberry cotoneaster (red berries)
Hardy pampas grass
Heavy metal switchgrass

Karl Foerster reed grass
Maidengrass
Oregon grape
Red twig dogwood (red bark)
Shrub roses (rose hips)
Specialty conifers

WORST

Arnold's Red honeysuckle
Holly (Ilex)

Rhododendron
Ribbon grass

ROSE GARDEN
BEST AND WORST LISTS

ROSES

HYBRID TEAS
- Black Garnett
- Lemon Spice (fragrant)
- Mister Lincoln
- Oklahoma
- Pascali
- Pristine
- Timeless (fragrant)
- Yankee Doodle

FLORIBUNDAS
- Europeana
- Gene Boerner
- Ivory Fashion
- Redgold
- Sunfire
- Sunsprite

GRANDIFLORAS
- Camelot
- Gold Medal
- Prima Donna

MINIATURES
- Baby Ophelia
- Cupcake
- Green Ice
- Magic Carrousel
- Single's Better

- Mary Marshal
- Rainbow's End
- Valerie Jean

CLIMBERS
- Altissimo
- America
- Blaze
- Golden Showers
- New Dawn
- White Dawn
- Zephirine Drouhin

MINIATURE CLIMBERS
- Jeanne Lajoie
- Ruby Pendant

OLD GARDEN SHRUB AND SPECIES ROSES
- Applejack (Shrub) (huge)
- Blush Damask (Damask)
- Celestial (Alba) (once-blooming)
- Crested Jewel (Moss) (one long blooming)
- Dortmund (Kordesii)
- Fruhlingsmorgen (Hybrid Spinosissima)
- Gertrude Jekyll (English)
- Golden Wings (Shrub)
- Graham Thomas (English)
- Hansa
- Henry Hudson (Hybrid Rugosa)
- Jens Munk (Hybrid Rugosa)
- Lilian Austin (Shrub)
- Linda Campbell (Hybrid Rugosa)
- Morden Centennial (Shrub)
- Mme. Hardy (Damask)
- Morden Blush (Alba)
- Paul Neyron (Hybrid Perpetual)
- Rosa Eglanteria (Species)
- Rosa Glauca (Species)
- Rosa Rugosa Rubra (or Alba Rugosa)
- Sally Holmes (Shrub)
- Sydonie (Hybrid Perpetual)
- William Baffin (Kordesii) (huge)

WORST

HYBRID TEAS
- Blue Girl
- Medallion
- Sterling Silver

CLIMBERS
- Dorothy Perkins (mildew-prone)

CLIMBERS
- Paul's Scarlet

MINIATURES
- Black Jade
- Judy Fischer
- Rose Window

OLD GARDEN
- Souv. de la Malmaison (winter tender)
- Suzanne (spreads uncontrollably)

LISTS · 145

GREAT ORNAMENTAL GRASSES, BULBS AND ROCK GARDEN PLANTS

GREAT ORNAMENTAL GRASSES

Big bluestem grass
Blue avena grass
Blue lyme grass
Feather reed grass

Fountain grass
Hardy pampas grass
Heavy metal switchgrass
Japanese blood grass

Maiden grass
Miscanthus grass
Overdam reed grass
Zebra grass

GREAT BULBS

Allium
Autumn crocus
Bearded iris
Begonias
Cannas
Crocosmia

Daffodils
Dahlias
Daylilies
Gladiolus
Gregeii tulip
Hyacinths

Lily-of-the-valley
Ranunculas
Siberian iris
Species tulip

GREAT ROCK GARDEN PLANTS

ANNUALS
Alyssum
Dianthus
Dwarf Alaskan pinpoint iris
Moss rose
Muscari hyacinths
Summer flowering vinca

BULBS
Crocus
Daffodils
Species tulips

PERENNIALS
Basket of gold
Bergenia
Bitterroot
Blue-eyed grass
Clump potentilla
Coral carpet sedum
Creeping baby's breath
Creeping phlox
Dalmatian bellflower
Draba
Dwarf hairy penstemon
Dwarf shasta daisy
Easter daisy
Gentian
German saponaria
Germander
Globularia

Harebell
Heronsbill
Little picklos
Miniature snow-in-summer
Perennial candytuft
Polish soapwort
Pussytoes
Staghorn potentilla
Rock cress
Rocky Mountain zinnia
Saxifrage
Self heal
Siberian skullcap
Silver sage
Stomatium
Sun rose
Wooly thyme

GREAT GROUND COVERS AND GREAT VINES AND CLIMBERS

GROUND COVERS

Ajuga
Creeping baby's breath
Basket of gold
Cotoneasters
Creeping buttercup
Creeping cinquefoil
Creeping junipers
Creeping phlox
Creeping rosemary
Creeping Verna potentilla
Flower carpet pink (rose)
Germander
Ground ivy
Hardy yellow iceplant
Hens and chicks
Japanese spurge
Kew euonymus
Kinnickinnick (mountains)
Lemon thyme
Mat penstemon
Moneywort
Mountain sandwort
Northern anemone
Miniature mat daisy
Mock strawberry
Oregon grape holly
Pearlwort
Purpleleaf
Pussytoes
Silver mound
Silver sage
Snow-in-Summer
Snow-on-the-Mountain
Soapwort
Sweet woodruff
Veronica
Vinca minor and major
Wintercreeper
Wooly thyme

VINES AND CLIMBERS

American bittersweet
Chinese wisteria
Clematis
Climbing hydrangea
Dutchman's pipe
Englemen ivy
English ivy
Five leaf akebia
Four-o'clocks
Honeysuckle
Lavender wisteria
Morning glory
Native hop vine
Silverlace vine
Sweet potato vine
Trumpet creeper
Trumpet vine
Variegated porcelain ampelopsis
Virginia creeper

WHAT BLOOMS WHEN CALENDAR

SPRING

ANNUALS
Bachelor button L
Dianthus L
Snapdragon L
Stock L

BULBS
Anemone,
 pasque flower M-L
Allium M-L
Crocus A
Daffodil M-L
Hyacinth A
Iris L
Tulip M-L

PERENNIALS
Ajuga L
Astilbe L
Baby's breath M-L
Bleeding heart,
 dwarf L
Candytuft L
Columbine L
Creeping phlox A
Daisy, sun A
Dead nettle L
Dianthus L
Draba A
Dutchman's pipe L
Five leaf akebia E
Flax, blue L
Fleabane A
Forget-me-not L
Gazania L
Geranium,
 cranesbill L
Geum L
Globeflower L
Gloxinia M-L
Guara L
Honeysuckle A
Kale L
Kinnickinnick L
Lamb's ear L
Leopard's bane M-L
Lily-of-the-valley L
Lupine L
Oregon grape holly E
Penstemon L
Polygonum L
Poppy L
Potentilla,
 creeping Verna L
Primrose L
Sea pink L
Snow-in-Summer L
Snow-on-the-mtn. L
Soapwort L
Spiderwort, blue L
Spurge L
Strawberry L
Sweet woodruff L
Verbena L
Veronica M-L
Viola A
Wisteria M-L

SUMMER

ANNUALS
Ageratum A
Alyssum A
Celosia A
Cosmos M-L
Four o'clock A
Gazania A
Geranium A
Impatiens E-L
Kale E
Lobelia M-L
Marigold A
Morning glory E-M
Moss rose A
Nasturtium M-L
Nicotiana M-L
Petunia A
Salvia A
Scabiosa A
Strawflower M-L
Sunflower M-L
Zinnia M-L

BULBS
Anemone, Japanese
 windflower L
Begonia A
Dahlia M-L
Daylily A
Gladiola A
Iris E

PERENNIALS
Aster E-M
Astilbe M-L
Balloon flower A
Baby's breath M-L
Bee balm E-M
Bellflower M-L
Black-eyed
 Susan M-L
Black snakeroot A
Bleeding heart,
 dwarf A
Candytuft E
Clematis A
Climbing
 hydrangea L
Columbine E-M
Coneflower M-L
Coral bells A
Coreopsis A
Cornflower E-M
Daisy, painted E-M
Daisy, shasta A
Daisy, sun A
Delphinium A
Dianthus E
Flax, blue E-M
Fleabane E-M
Forget-me-not E
Foxglove A
Gaillardia A
Gloxinia E
Gayfeather M-L
Geranium,
 cranesbill E-M
Geum E-M
Globeflower E
Harebell A
Hollyhock A
Honeysuckle A

148 - MONTH-TO-MONTH GARDENING

WHAT BLOOMS WHEN CALENDAR

SUMMER

PERENNIALS
Hosta M-L
Hyssop M-L
Jacob's ladder E-M
Jupiter's beard A
Lady's mantle E-M
Lamb's ear E
Lavender M-L
Leadwort M-L
Ligularia M-L
Lily M-L
Lupine E-M
Maltese cross E-M
Meadow rue E-M
Moneywort E-M
Monkshood A
Dead nettle E-M
Obedient plant M-L
Penstemon A
Peony E
Phlox,
   tall garden M-L
Pincushion flower A
Polygonum A
Poppy Mallow A
Poppy A
Potentilla A
Primrose A
Pussytoes E
Red hot poker L
Red valerian A
Rock cress E
Sage A
Silverlace vine L
Santolina A
Sea pink E
Sedum A
Snow-in-Summer E
Snow-on-the-
   mountain E
Soapwort E
Starflower L
Spiderwort E-M
Strawberry A
Sun rose M-L
Sweet Woodruff E
Thyme A
Trumpet
   creeper M-L
Trumpet vine M-L
Verbena A
Veronica A
Vinca minor A
Whirling
   Butterflies A
Yarrow A

FALL

ANNUALS
Cosmos E
Kale A
Marigold A
Morning glory E
Moss rose E-M
Zinnia A

BULBS
Canna E
Dahlia E-M

PERENNIALS
Aster E
Black-eyed Susan E-M
Bleeding heart,
   dwarf A
Bubblemint E
Clematis E-M
Coneflower E
Coral bells E
Coreopsis E
Daisy A
Engleman ivy A
Foxglove E
Gaillardia E
Gayflower E
Gazania E
Harebell E
Helen's Flower E-M
Honeysuckle E-M
Leadwort E-M
Liatris E-M
Ligularia E
Mum E-M
Obedient plant E-M
Polygonum E
Poppy E
Poppy Mallow E-M
Primrose E-M
Red hot poker E-M
Red valerian E
Sage A
Sedum E
Silverlace vine A
Spurge A
Starflower E-M
Sunrose E
Tiger lily E
Trumpet creeper E
Trumpet vine E
Turtlehead E-M
Verbena E
Veronica A
Vinca minor E
Viola A
Whirling
   butterflies E
Yarrow E

*A – blooms All season
*E – blooms Early in the season
*L – blooms Late in the season
*M – blooms Mid-season

**Plants listed in all seasons are often different varieties of the same plant. Check with your garden center to see when each variety blooms.

LAWN MAINTENANCE CALENDAR

January	Water if snowfall is minimal, and only if soil is not frozen. Do not water on top of snow. Water between 10 a.m. and 2 p.m. and only for brief periods, no longer than 15 minutes.
February	Same as January.
March	Check irrigation system. Apply pre-emergent* by April 15.
April	Apply pre-emergent* before April 15. Apply ½ to 1 pound nitrogen per 1,000 square feet of bluegrass lawn. Core aeration recommended for heavily compacted lawns, or lawns with more than ½" of thatch. Mow to 2" to 2½" during spring.
May	Increase watering amounts and begin to water in early morning hours between 4 a.m. and 7 a.m. Water approximately 1" per week.
June	Fertilize with ½ to 1 pound nitrogen per 1,000 square feet of bluegrass lawn before June 15. Do not fertilize if clippings are returned to the lawn with a mulching mower. Do not fertilize if temperatures exceed 95° for more than 10 days in a row. Water approximately 1" to 1½" per week. Mow lawn to 2½" to 3" (highest mower setting) during summer.
July	Check watering on south and west slopes. Maintain adequate watering this month. No fertilizer is needed now. Water approximately 1½" to 2" per week.
August	Same as July except water approximately 2" per week.
September	Apply ½ to 1 pound nitrogen per 1,000 square feet of bluegrass lawn. Core aerate if thatch or compaction is a problem. Water approximately 1½" to 2" per week. Mow to 2" to 2½" during the fall.
October	Apply ½ to 1 pound nitrogen per 1,000 square feet of bluegrass lawn. Using a winterizer fertilizer is appropriate now. Decrease water to lawn.
November	Same as January.
December	Same as January.

HOW TO IDENTIFY LAWN INSECTS AND DISEASES / Unexplained brown spots or thinning in lawn may be due to disease or insects. Take a sample and description to your local garden center or call your county extension office.

PREVENTATIVE MEASURES AGAINST LAWN DISEASES / Don't water in the evenings; don't over or under fertilize; aerate your lawn; once you note a problem with your lawn, take care of it immediately before the disease or fungus spreads.

HOW TO CONTROL LAWN INSECTS / Chemical treatment is only necessary when insect population is high. There are new methods of organic controls. Talk to your local garden center or call your county extension office.

* Most pre-emergents work by creating a chemical barrier for seeds. If that barrier is established before the seed germinates, the seed will die before it breaks through the soil. That is why it is so important to apply the pre-emergent at the correct time, which is before the seed can germinate. To prevent crabgrass, apply a pre-emergent before the soil temperature reaches 55° (early spring).

CHILES YOU CAN GROW IN COLORADO

CHILE	AVERAGE SIZE	AVERAGE HEAT
Nu Mex R. Naky	6"	Mild
Big Jim	12"	Mild/medium
Chimayo	6"	Medium
Española Improved	5"	Medium
New Mexico 64	7"	Medium
Sandia	6"	Medium/hot
Jalapeño	3" to 4"	Medium hot/hot
De Arbol	2" to 4"	Hot
Mirasol	3" to 4"	Hot
Serrano	2" to 4"	Hot
Habanero	1" to 3"	Very, very hot
Ancho	4" to 5"	Good for rellenos

ZONE MAP

There are two primary zones in Colorado: Zone 4 for the mountain areas (Zone 3 in the really high elevations) and Zone 5 for the rest of Colorado. Conservatively, Zone 5 areas have a growing season of approximately 105 days, while Zone 4 has a growing season of approximately 70 days. You're safe from frost after May 15 in Zone 5 and after about June 15 in Zone 4.

If you are unsure about what the gardening zone is where you live, check with a garden center near you.

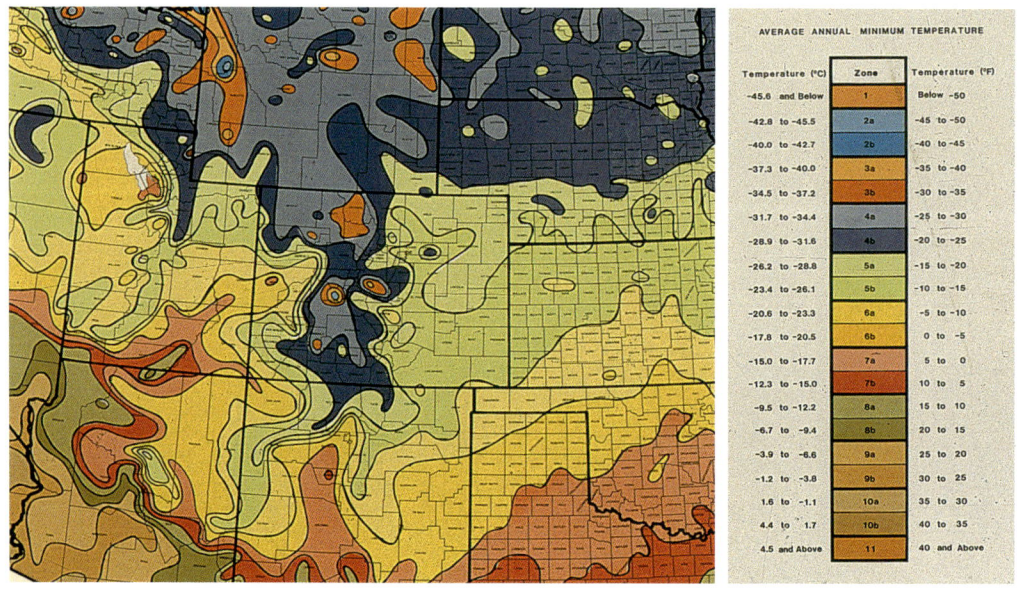

Map courtesy of Agricultural Research Service, USDA

NOTES

INDEX

A

AERATE: 15, 19, 21, 22, 53, 59, 150
ALLIUM: 18
AMARYLLIS: 66, 62
AMENDING: 83, 85, 97, 101, 104
  How To Amend: 127
ANNUALS: 7, 13, 45
  buying: 7
  deadhead: 33, 38, 44
  fertilizing: 16, 33, 44
  watering: 124
  weeding: 123
APHIDS: 105
ASTERS: 6

B

BABY'S BREATH: 19
BACHELOR'S BUTTON: 19
BACILLUS THURINGIENSIS (BT): 129
BERM: 30
BIRD FEEDER: 72
BIRDS: 73
BLOOD MEAL: 26
BULBS: 146
  dividing: 33, 51
  forced: 65, 66
BUTTERFLIES: 38, 39

C

CALIFORNIA POPPY: 19, 51
CANNAS: 13, 18, 33, 57, 59
CATERPILLARS: 36
CHILE PEPPERS: 26, 46, 151
CHRISTMAS CACTUS: 71
CLIMBERS: 147
COLD FRAMES: 8
COLEUS: 34
COMPOST: 61
  hot: 60
  How To: 111
  winter: 73
CRABGRASS: 15, 123, 150
COSMOS: 23, 51
CROCUS: 33, 57, 65

D

DAFFODIL: 57, 59, 65
DAHLIA: 13, 18, 33, 57, 59
DAYLILY: 51
DEADHEADING: 44
  How To: 112
DIANTHUS: 6
DISEASES
  black spot: 129
  lawn: 129
  oyster shell scale: 10
  powdery mildew: 129
  scale: 129
  tree: 129
DUTCH IRIS: 65
DWARF IRIS: 65

F

FERTILIZING: 13, 14, 16, 21, 25, 35, 40, 44, 58
  How To: 114
  roses: 114
  slow-release: 77
FLOWERING TOBACCO: 34
FLOWERS
  cutting: 42
  drying: 44
  edible: 41
FORSYTHIA: 43
FRUIT
  pears: 53
  strawberries: 20

INDEX

G

GARDEN GIFT BASKET: 72
GARLIC: 46, 54, 59, 117
GAZANIA: 34
GERANIUM: 34
GLADIOLUS: 13, 18, 33, 57, 59
GRASS: 54
GRASS
  blue gramma: 35
  buffalograss: 35, 85
  cool season: 54
    bluegrass: 22, 26
    fescues: 22, 26
  Kentucky bluegrass: 85
  maintenance: 150
  ornamental: 7, 24, 146
GREENHOUSES: 8
GROUND COVERS: 20, 147

H

HELIOTROPE: 34
HERBICIDES: 37
HERBS: 41, 45, 54, 55, 117
  basil: 27
  best: 139
  chives: 27, 46
  dill: 27, 46
  drying: 54
  garden: 76
  mint: 46
  oregano: 46
  parsley: 27, 46
  rosemary: 46
  sage: 46
  thyme: 46
HOUSEPLANTS: 17, 76
  How To Clean: 111
HUMMINGBIRDS: 38
HYACINTHS: 33, 57, 65

I

INSECTS
  aphids: 10, 14, 23, 105, 125, 129
  cabbage butterflies: 47
  control of: 129
  fungus gnats: 129
  grasshoppers: 41
  lawn: 129
  lawn maintenance: 150
  mealy bugs: 129
  mites: 14
  pine beetle: 105
  pine tip moth: 129
  slugs: 41
  snails: 41
  spider mites: 42, 43, 47, 129
  tobacco budworm: 39
  tomato hornworms: 47, 48
  white pine weevil: 105
  whiteflies: 129
IRRIGATION SYSTEMS: 21, 58, 65

L

LARKSPUR: 19
LILACS: 43
LILIES: 18
LOVE-IN-A-MIST: 51

M

MARIGOLD: 6, 27
MICROCLIMATE: 104
MULCHING
  How To: 115
  mulch: 14, 23, 25, 28, 57, 58, 60, 62
MUMS: 23, 38, 51

INDEX

N
NASTURTIUM: 27

O
ORIENTAL POPPY: 38

P
PANSIES: 13, 19, 51, 57
PAPERWHITE: 66
PEONIES: 51, 52
PERENNIALS: 18, 56, 62, 99
  buying: 7
  deadheading: 33, 38, 44
  dividing: 19
  fertilizing: 33
  watering: 124
  weeding: 123
PETUNIAS: 6
POINSETTIA: 42, 55, 70, 71
PRUNING: 7, 9, 15, 20
  How To: 119
  vines: 9

R
RABBITS: 27
ROSES: 14, 15, 21, 36, 44, 64
  garden: 90-91
  How To Plant and Transplant: 118
  mounded: 70
  watering: 124

S
SALSA: 46
SALSA GARDEN: 26
SEEDS: 52
  catalogs: 72, 74, 87
  indoors: 8
  testing: 6
  vegetable: 74
  wildflower: 56

SHADE GARDEN: 144
SHRUBS: 119, 120, 135, 136
  Best: 138
  Checklist: 135
  deciduous: 7, 119, 139
  How To Plant and Transplant: 120
  lilacs: 24
  mulches: 21
  shopping for: 137
  watering: 124, 138
SNAPDRAGON: 19
SPRINKLER SYSTEMS: 58

T
THATCH: 40
TOOLS
  cleaning: 64, 72
  sharpening: 10
  storing: 64
TOPIARY FLOWERS: 74
TRANSPLANTING: 13, 51, 52, 120
TREES: 136
  aspens: 10
  best: 138
  bonsai: 69
  checklist: 135
  Christmas: 63, 69, 70, 71
  create a miniature orchard: 120
  deciduous: 14, 119, 139
  diseases: 129
  evergreens: 14, 53, 119
  How To Plant and Transplant: 120
  How To Stake: 122
  juniper: 15
  leaves: 58
  maple: 14
  shopping for: 137
  watering: 124, 138
  wisteria: 14
TULIPS: 33, 57, 65

INDEX

U

UTILITY NOTIFICATION CENTER: 29

V

VEGETABLES
 beans: 27, 46, 54
 broccoli: 8, 16, 28, 116
 brussel sprouts: 54, 59, 116
 cabbage: 8, 16, 41, 54, 75, 86
 carrots: 16, 29, 54, 60, 116
 chile peppers: 117
 cucumbers: 27, 46, 54, 117
 eggplant: 8
 gourds: 59, 60
 How To Harvest: 116
 kale: 16
 lettuce: 16, 36, 116
 onions: 16, 116
 peas: 16, 36, 116
 peppers: 27, 46, 47, 117
 pole beans: 117
 potatoes: 65, 116
 pumpkins: 27, 59
 radishes: 16, 27, 36, 117
 spinach: 16, 36, 116
 squash: 45, 59
  winter squash: 60
 tomatillos: 116
 tomatoes: 8, 27, 28, 41, 45, 47, 54, 116
 zucchini: 27, 47, 54, 117
VINES: 29, 147
VIOLAS: 51

W

WATERING: 37
 guide: 124
 How To Deep Water: 113
 interior plants: 124
 lawn: 150
 winter: 78
WEEDING: 37
 How To Weed: 123
WILDLIFE: 63
 How To Keep Away Deer and Elk: 112
WINDOWBOX: 24, 96, 97
WINTER: 75
 Best and Worst List: 144

X

XERISCAPE: 84-85
 Best and Worst List: 140

Z

ZINNIA: 23, 27
ZONES: 152

INDEX - 157

ORDER FORM

MONTH-TO-MONTH GARDENING COLORADO
4340 E. KENTUCKY AVE., Suite 446
DENVER, CO 80246
888-456-3607

PLEASE SEND ME: Price   Quantity

MONTH-TO-MONTH GARDENING COLORADO $19.95   _____
MONTH-TO-MONTH GARDENING NEW MEXICO $16.95   _____
MONTH-TO-MONTH GARDENING UTAH $16.95   _____

SUBTOTAL: $ _____

Colorado residents add 3.8% sales tax. $ _____

Add $4.50 for shipping for 1st book, add $1 for each additional $ _____

TOTAL ENCLOSED: $ _____

SEND TO:

Name _____

Address _____

City _____ State _____ Zip _____

Gift From _____

We accept checks, money orders, Visa or Mastercard (please include expiration date). Please make checks payable to 3D Press, Inc. Sorry, no COD orders.

Please charge my   ☐ VISA   ☐ MASTERCARD

Card Number _____ Expiration Date _____

Cardholder's Signature _____

CALL TOLL FREE 888-456-3607 FOR MORE INFORMATION